Dr. Wim Malgo

Called to Pray

How to Be a Prayer Warrior

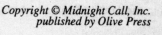

Preface

Dr. Wim Malgo, the Founder of Midnight Call Ministries, went home to be with the Lord on August 8th, 1992. While he had the gift of interpreting the prophetic Word, his strongest avenue in the ministry was prayer. In August of 1971, he wrote this book: *Called To Pray—How To Be A Prayer Warrior*, which has been translated into many different languages and no doubt has become the backbone of this very blessed ministry of Midnight Call.

This all-important and powerful book deals exclusively with prayer, the only weapon for Christians in a world full of darkness.

—Arno Froese, Director
Midnight Call U.S.A.

Table of Contents

CHAPTER 1

The Enemies of Prayer

"I exhort therefore, that, first of all, supplications, prayers, intercessions, and giving of thanks, be made for all men; for kings, and for all that are in authority; that we may lead a quiet and peaceable life in all godliness and honesty. For this is good and acceptable in the sight of God our Savior; who will have all men to be saved, and to come unto the knowledge of the truth" (1st Timothy 2:1–4).

There are six terrible weapons which the devil uses to clip the prayer wings of God's children:

1. Fatigue!

This is the paralyzing fatigue which makes you incapable of persevering in prayer. And yet, prayer is the best way of overcoming this unnatural fatigue, for the Bible says, *"He giveth power to the faint; and to them that have no might he increaseth strength... But they that wait upon the LORD shall renew their strength; they shall mount up with wings as eagles; they shall run, and not be weary; and they shall walk, and not faint"* (Isaiah 40:29, 31). Cast yourself into the river of prayer, for there you will find true refreshment.

2. Distraction!

You are unable to concentrate. Other thoughts are constantly coming into your mind. During prayer you suddenly realize with horror that your thoughts are occupied with something quite different. This weapon of the enemy is made ineffective through praying aloud. David says in Psalm 55:16–17, *"As for me, I will call upon God; and the LORD shall save me. Evening, and morning, and at noon, will I pray, and cry aloud: and he shall hear my voice."* Pray aloud and audibly, child of God, and then the powers of distraction will have no influence over you!

3. Inner Restlessness!

An inexplicable restlessness grips you. You can only be freed of this kind of restlessness by praying.

Whatever the cause may be, whether it is sin, nervousness, or unbelief—the Bible says, *"Cast thy burden upon the LORD, and he shall sustain thee: he shall never suffer the righteous to be moved"* (Psalm 55:22). And furthermore we read, *"Why art thou cast down, O my soul? and why art thou disquieted within me? hope thou in God: for I shall yet praise him, who is the health of my countenance, and my God"* (Psalm 42:11). Only by praying will you receive help in this respect also.

4. Haste!

The weapon which Satan probably uses most successfully with many who want to pray is haste. What does the Scripture say in Ecclesiastes 8:3? *"Be not hasty to go out of his sight...."* What is the reason for your haste? The amount of work you have! You can see no end to your work. But in prayer and only in prayer will the conditions be present in which you can do your work most effectively and efficiently. The longer you pray, the more work you will accomplish. I know that this is contrary to all our reasoning, but a thousandfold experience confirms it and the Bible says it in Isaiah 55:2, *"Wherefore do ye spend money for that which is not bread? and your labour for that which satisfieth not? hearken diligently unto me, and eat ye that which is good, and let your soul delight itself in fatness."* By persevering in prayer, your daily work load will be undergirded by divine resources of power. To your surprise you will discover that the time which you spent in earnest prayer was a most profitable time, and the terrible weapon of haste has been blunted.

5. Despair!

Despair is a weapon which paralyzes many praying Christians. Despair means not looking far enough ahead. The Bible says, "Look... unto Jesus." This looking to Jesus implies that we should take our eyes off the visible and look to Jesus—look to Him in prayer!

You may be in despair over your weakness, in despair over your defeats, in despair over the hardness of men's hearts, or in despair over sad circumstances. Paul calls out in 2nd

Corinthians 4:8, *"We are troubled on every side, yet not distressed; we are perplexed, but not in despair."* Why? Because he prayed! Isaiah says, *"Strengthen ye the weak hands, and confirm the feeble knees. Say to them that are of a fearful heart, Be strong, fear not: behold, your God will come with vengeance, even God with a recompence; he will come and save you"* (Isaiah 35:3–4).

There is only one way of being freed of despair: that is by earnest prayer. As I write this, I feel as if unseen powers are trying to keep me from writing the facts as they are. I know that Satan will attempt in every way to make you so despondent that you cannot believe that prayer can unlock God's eternal resources of power. But in the name of Jesus, these powers also are conquered. I would like to call to those with despairing hearts: Pray! Make a new beginning today! Say aloud: "I choose the will of God and in the name of Jesus, I reject the will of Satan!" It is the will of God that you pray. The will of Satan is that you do not pray.

6. Indolence!

This is a tricky weapon which Satan uses against those who want to become men and women of prayer. It is the weapon of indolence—laziness of the flesh, of weakness. You get down on your knees, you want to pray, but you can hardly utter a word. Everything is so difficult. The flesh is not able to pray.

How can you be freed of this terrible indolence, this weakness? Here is the answer: Pray with the Bible. Read over and over, and aloud, the promises which deal with prayer. Jesus has said, *"Ask, and it shall be given you; seek, and ye shall find; knock, and it shall be opened unto you*" (Matthew 7:7).

Simply tell the Lord in prayer: "Lord, I cannot ask, but You say in Your Word that I should do it, unceasingly."

Tell Him all your problems. Do not be silent! And while you are speaking with Him about it and reading His Word, you will suddenly notice a spark of prayer will light up inside you. Your indolence will disappear and you can break through to the throne of grace!

CHAPTER 2

Hindrances to Prayer

"And when ye spread forth your hands, I will hide mine eyes from you: yea, when ye make many prayers, I will not hear: your hands are full of blood" (Isaiah 1:15).

Hindrance #1– Hands Stained With Blood

Perhaps someone is saying now, "I still do not have a spirit of prayer. I cannot really pray." In this case, there must be serious obstacles to prayer in your life, things which paralyze your prayer wings.

In our text, the Lord says in effect, "I will not hear your prayers because your hands are stained with blood."

We read the same in Isaiah 59:1 and the following verse, *"Behold, the LORD'S hand is not shortened, that it cannot save; neither his ear heavy, that it cannot hear: But your iniquities have separated between you and your God, and your sins have hid his face from you, that he will not hear."*

Here we have the first obstacle to prayer. One whose hands are stained with blood is a murderer. Are your hands

stained with blood? "No!" you answer. Do not say this too
quickly. The Bible says, *"Whosoever hateth his brother is a
murderer..."* (1st John 3:15). If there is any sort of grudge in
your heart against another person, your hands are stained
with blood. God turns away from you when you pray. You
can feel it too: The heavens seem like brass, you cannot get
through.

So I ask you earnestly: Go and make peace with your
brother or your sister. You will experience how the Spirit of
prayer will be poured out on you and you will become a
praying Christian.

Hindrance#2– Lying Lips

The second hindrance which prevents God's hearing your
prayers is found in Isaiah 59:3, *"...your lips have spoken lies,
your tongue hath muttered perverseness."* Have you never
noticed how an urge can come over you and virtually compel
you to say negative things about others when you are
together with people? Have you not sometimes said terrible
things about a minister of the Gospel to a fellow Christian?
You have thereby touched one of the Lord's anointed!
Spiritual slander is a terrible thing.   *I don't want to*

For example, I may enjoy genuine fellowship and have a
deep respect for a certain brother. Then someone comes to *slander*
me and tells me something negative about his life. The
moment I hear this, the invisible bond of fellowship between
him and me is broken.

When I meet him again, I am as friendly as before but in
my heart there is the venom of slander. He can sense it, but

he is powerless to do anything about it because he does not know what was said about him.

How often have you harmed the good reputation of another through gossip which you cannot prove? Remember, this is an abomination to the Lord. You can pray as much as you want, but the Lord will close the heavens above you, as long as you do not repent of this gossip and rectify the situation. If you are sure that someone is on the wrong road, then speak to the Lord about it and with the person concerned, but do not repeat it to another. In Psalm 15:1 and 3 it says, *"LORD, who shall abide in thy tabernacle? who shall dwell in thy holy hill? ...He that backbiteth not with his tongue, nor doeth evil to his neighbour, nor taketh up a reproach against his neighbour."* I implore you—repent of the sins of your tongue. Renounce this spirit of gossip, for the Bible says, *"In the multitude of words there wanteth not sin: but he that refraineth his lips is wise"* (Proverbs 10:19). You should be a prayer warrior!

Hindrance#3–Marital Discord

The third hindrance to prayer is described for us in 1st Peter 3:6–7, *"Even as Sara obeyed Abraham, calling him lord: whose daughters ye are, as long as ye do well, and are not afraid with any amazement. Likewise, ye husbands, dwell with them according to knowledge, giving honour unto the wife, as unto the weaker vessel, and as being heirs together of the grace of life; that your prayers be not hindered."* Married people, your prayers are hindered if something is wrong in your marriage.

Sara called her husband Abraham, "lord," but she still had an equal part in God's grace. The woman is to be subject to her husband, for he is the head just as Christ is the head of the Church (see Ephesians 5:22–25).

However, this does not mean that the husband is entitled to be a tyrant or dictator—on the contrary: In 1st Peter 3:7 the husband is admonished to honour his wife, so that his prayers will not be hindered. All tensions and problems in marriage are a result of the fact that the Lord Jesus Christ, the Crucified One, does not stand between the two people concerned.

Happy are the marriage partners for whom Jesus is the center. If differences of opinion arise and the two "I's" threaten to collide, Jesus stands between them, and in Him they always find each other again. The wife adopts her proper attitude toward her husband because she loves him, and the husband towards his wife because they both love the Lord. I would ask you married people— "Are you leading your married life in such a way that your prayers are not hindered?" If not, repent! Do it quickly! Time is short!

Hindrance#4—Disobedience

The fourth very serious hindrance to prayer is disobedience. In Proverbs 28:9 it says, *"He that turneth away his ear from hearing the law, even his prayer shall be abomination."* The law is the Word of God. The Lord says here, in effect, "He who closes his ear, the ear of his heart, to hearing the Word (Biblical hearing means to respond to the Word by obeying it), his prayer is an abomination." John says with bold confidence, *"And whatsoever we ask, we receive of him..."*

(1st John 3:22). Why? *"...because we keep his command-ments, and do those things that are pleasing in his sight."*

But, I have repeatedly experienced in services that when the Holy Spirit was pointing His sword at believers and I then gave an opportunity to pray, many of God's children turned this sword back to God and said to the Lord, in effect, "Yes, Lord, please work obedience in me." Actually, what you are saying is, "Lord, if I then do not become obedi-ent, it will be your fault!"

This is why you do not make any headway—why you do not become a person of prayer—because you are quite willing to be religious and to pray piously, but without becoming obedient in actual practice. Do not think that God is inter-ested in your theological expositions in your prayers. He is not interested in your lamentations, or even in your tears. God is interested in your obedience! *"...to obey is better than sacrifice..."* (1st Samuel 15:22).

Now you will perhaps answer, "Doesn't God work in me 'both to will and to do' His good pleasure?" He will give you this the moment He makes His Word alive in you through the Holy Spirit.

I would ask you now in the presence of God: "Will you become obedient? Will you now do what He is asking of you?" If you say "Yes!" to this with all your heart, you too will become a prayer warrior. You will not only ask, but you will also receive in faith!

CHAPTER 3

The Conditions for Answered Prayer

*"Hear my prayer, O LORD, and let my cry come unto thee...
He will regard the prayer of the destitute, and not despise
their prayer"* (Psalm 102:1 and 17).

First, we should ask ourselves: "What is the real inner condition for victorious prayer?"

Condition#1–To Be Poor and Afflicted

Search in the Scriptures and see how often the Lord
promises to help the poor and afflicted, and to hear their
prayer. *"And the afflicted people thou wilt save..."* (2nd
Samuel 22:28). *"For the LORD saw the affliction of Israel..."*
(2nd Kings 14:26). *"[He]...giveth right to the poor"* (Job 36:6).
"LORD, thou hast heard the desire of the humble..." (Psalm
10:17). *"This poor man cried, and the LORD heard him..."*
(Psalm 34:6). Yes, it even says in Psalm 149:4, *"...the LORD*

taketh pleasure in his people: he will beautify the meek with salvation." We could go on and on!

We must be powerless, despairing of ourselves. Only such people can become powerful prayer warriors, for true prayer is the expression of greatest dependence upon the Lord. All those who still do not know how to pray effectively are people whose own strength is hindering the power of the Lord. I always feel somewhat apprehensive when I hear people pray, "Lord please give me power," for our Lord has no use for powerful people.

The feeling of strength drives away the Spirit of prayer. The Bible says, *"...my strength is made perfect in weakness..."* (2nd Corinthians 12:9), and *"...the LORD is the strength of my life..."* (Psalm 27:1). Thus, only those who are weak in themselves can pray properly. Here I want to say to all my readers who are ill, elderly or unable to work: "You especially, can be men and women of prayer!"

Condition#2–To Be Forsaken

Psalm 102:17 says, *"He will regard the prayer of the destitute, and not despise their prayer."* This verse refers to lonely and forsaken people.

If you have had bitter disappointments from fellow Christians and fellow men, yes, if even the dearest one you have on this Earth has disappointed you, then God has permitted this because He wants to make you a person of prayer.

Let me say it more clearly: God takes away all your human props, so that you can become increasingly dependent on Him alone. The Bible says, *"...Cursed be the man*

that trusteth in man, and maketh flesh his arm, ...[But]
*Blessed is the man that trusteth in the LORD, and whose
hope the LORD is"* (Jeremiah 17:5 and 7). It is essential that
you become disillusioned with flesh and blood so that the
Spirit of prayer can come over you with power. This is reason
enough to think lovingly of those who have disappointed you.

Then we need to ask ourselves, "What must be our position before God in prayer?" Here, too, Scripture speaks very
clearly: *"The LORD is far from the wicked: but he heareth the
prayer of the righteous"* (Proverbs 15:29). *"...The effectual fervent prayer of a righteous man availeth much"* (James 5:16).
Yes, wretched and weak in myself, yet perfect, justified, and
immaculate I may come and stand before the holy presence
of God! How is this possible? It is only possible through the
blood of Jesus. According to Romans 3:25, we obtain the
righteousness which is valid before God through the blood of
Jesus. Thus, we can come before the throne of God only
through the holy blood. *"Having therefore, brethren, boldness
to enter into the holiest by the blood of Jesus..."* (Hebrews
10:19). This tremendous fact is so often overlooked. We can
never speak to God without going through the blood of Jesus
in the Spirit.

Why do you feel so constricted when you pray? Because
you forget that you must come through the blood of Jesus.
And we cannot come through the blood of Jesus unless the
Holy Spirit reveals the Lamb to us and unless we experience
something of His suffering for our sins, and unless we are
driven to worship and adoration. Why is this? It is because
the prerequisite for effective intercession is always adoration
and worship. Therefore, never come thoughtlessly into the

holy presence of God, for He hides Himself from you if you do not approach Him consciously through the blood of Jesus. Begin to worship the Father and the Son and you will see how your heart is opened and you can make intercession.

The Best Time to Pray

Let us ask ourselves further: "What is the best time to pray?" Many will say, "In the morning. Of course!" Scripture says, *"O God, thou art my God; early will I seek thee: my soul thirsteth for thee..."* (Psalms 63:1). Only those who have first had an encounter with the Victor will have victory during the day. What you are in your quiet time in the morning, you will be the whole day through.

We want to answer this question according to Scripture from yet another aspect. In Hebrews 4:16 we read, *"Let us therefore come boldly unto the throne of grace, that we may obtain mercy, and find grace to help in time of need."*

When are we in need of help? Always! We must do as it says in 1st Thessalonians 5:17, *"Pray without ceasing."* This is both direct and indirect prayer: Direct prayer in the quiet time and indirect prayer throughout the day.

The Benefits of Fellowship With the Lord

In these days when the world is contaminated by demonic powers, only those who have uninterrupted fellowship with the Lord will come through. In these endtimes, when temptations are becoming ever greater, only those who pray will experience the victory of the Lord.

In these last days of grace, as the darkness is gathering, only those who have learned to pray can walk in the light.

As this world becomes increasingly hardened, only those who pray can tear souls out of the devil's clutches!

Miracles happen when Christians pray,
As in faith they come to the throne,
Worlds can be conquered in this way,
And great is God's reward to His own.

Therefore, pray, pray, pray without ceasing!

CHAPTER 4

The Guarantee of Answered Prayer

"God is not a man, that he should lie; neither the son of man, that he should repent: hath he said, and shall he not do it? or hath he spoken, and shall he not make it good?" (Numbers 23:19).

Let us ask ourselves now: "What guarantee do we have that God really hears our prayers?"

God's Infallible Word

We must begin to take God's promises in the Bible seriously. Our real trouble is that we rely more on our feelings, on flesh and blood, on experiences and on our capabilities than we rely on the promises of God. This grieves the heart of our Lord, *"God is not a man, that he should lie; neither the son of man, that he should repent: hath he said, and shall he not do it? or hath he spoken, and shall he not make it good?"* (Numbers 23:19).

When Jesus says, *"Ask, and it shall be given you..."* (Matthew 7:7), He means what He says, and it is not an empty phrase. In prayer we may put our finger on such promises and say: "You have said it, O Lord!" And in His promises, we have the guarantee that He will hear us.

The Precious Name of Jesus

Jesus has told us this truth repeatedly: *"And whatsoever ye shall ask in my name, that will I do, that the Father may be glorified in the Son"* (John 14:13), and *"If ye shall ask any thing in my name, I will do it"* (verse 14). Is this not a clear promise? *"Whatsoever ye shall ask the Father in my name, he will give it you. Hitherto have ye asked nothing in my name: ask, and ye shall receive, that your joy may be full"* (John 16:23–24).

These three promises of Jesus tell us the following, if we ask the Father in His name:

- First, He will do it!
- Second, He will give it!
- Third, we shall receive it!

Thus, we have a three-fold promise that we shall be heard: He will do and give and we shall receive.

Therefore, child of God, learn this threefold prayer of increasing intensity, which Jesus encourages us to pray: *"Ask!"* This means to beg. *"Seek!"* This means persistency, striving towards the fulfillment of what has been asked. *"Knock!"* This means to assail Heaven's door vehemently. The wonderful thing about prayer is that by praying we are enabled to pray more fervently because God gives us the assurance in prayer that He will surely answer if we ask in the name of Jesus.

Now what is meant by "asking in the name of Jesus?" This is not only the cashing of a signed check which will be paid out to me in full, simply because the name of the One is written on it who has become the Heir of all things, but to ask in the name of Jesus also means to bring His name before God. Therewith I am saying "Yes!" to the name of Jesus, "Yes!" to the Redeemer, "Yes!" to His cross, and because God also says, "Yes!" to this name, God having fully accepted the vicarious sacrifice of Jesus, my request will be granted!

My will is fused with His holy will. This is what Jesus means when He says in John 15:7, *"If ye abide in me, and my words abide in you, ye shall ask what ye will, and it shall be done unto you."* Are you willing to abide in Him? Are you willing to submit yourself completely to His name? Is it your heartfelt desire to be one with Jesus?

If this is the case, a new possibility opens up for you which is known only to a few, namely, the working of the glory of God in and through your life in answer to your asking, *"Whatsoever ye shall ask in my name, I will do it."*

Our Own Sincerity

Hebrews 10:19 and onwards encourages us to enter into the holy place by the blood of Jesus, for we have a High Priest over the house of God.

Before we draw near to God we are warned, *"Let us draw near with a true heart..."* (Hebrews 10:22). Is your heart true?

When you ask the Lord to forgive a sin, are you also willing deep down in your heart to break with this sin, or do you extend one hand toward the Lord asking forgiveness and hold on to the sin with the other hand? In this case you are lying before His holy face!

If you pray and ask the Lord to send many laborers into His harvest so that the world can be reached with the Gospel, and you are not willing to go and to sacrifice yourself, then your prayer is a lie, it is hypocrisy! God says in His Word, *"He layeth up sound wisdom for the righteous..."* (Proverbs 2:7). You may ask the question: "How can I know whether I am really sincere in prayer or whether I am still untruthful?" There is one unmistakable sign: You are not truthful, if in religious self-satisfaction, you have a good opinion of yourself! You think that you always do your duty, that your life is pleasing to God, that you cannot be lacking in anything because you have a long-proven orthodox doctrine of faith. If you are satisfied with yourself in this manner, you can be sure that you are a liar, a hypocrite before God, for the Scripture says, *"If we say that we have no sin, we deceive ourselves, and the truth is not in us"* (1st John 1:8).

Sober Realization of Your Own Depravity

Thousands upon thousands of people in churches and congregations today pray in this hypocritically religious manner. However, only when you are convinced of your complete depravity, only when you have lost all faith in yourself, have you come into a truthful attitude of heart. *"For thus saith the high and lofty One that inhabiteth eternity, whose name is Holy; I dwell in the high and holy place, with him also that is of a contrite and humble spirit, to revive the spirit of the humble, and to revive the heart of the contrite ones"* (Isaiah 57:15).

Dear brethren, when you become men and women of prayer you will begin to know yourselves better. There are many who come to the Lord's table every Sunday who have been baptized in the Biblical way, many who know the pure, clear Word of God, but their own hearts they do not know, and therefore they are not truthful in prayer.

Untruthfulness is ingrained in our flesh and blood, but there is nothing more cleansing, more heart-searching than persevering prayer. Only in this attitude can I begin to see my sin as God sees it.

Only in His presence am I torn out of the old religious rut, out of dead formalities, and placed into living reality. Only then can I recognize with my spirit—and not with my intellect as I have previously done—the Lord Jesus, the truth! He says, *"...the truth shall make you free"* (John 8:32).

All the unloosed bonds, all the unanswered questions, all the stubborn, secret lusts which persist in your life of faith, they are there because you have not yet recognized the truth about yourself.

Therefore, I would ask you most sincerely to begin to seek the Lord with a willing, sincere heart as never before, and you will have the guarantee that you will be heard!

CHAPTER 5

The Prayer of Faith

"But without faith it is impossible to please him: for he that cometh to God must believe that he is, and that he is a rewarder of them that diligently seek him" (Hebrews 11:6). *"But let him ask in faith, nothing wavering. For he that wavereth is like a wave of the sea driven with the wind and tossed. For let not that man think that he shall receive any thing of the Lord"* (James 1:6–7).

Our next question is: "How must we pray?"

In Faith!

What does it mean to pray in faith? It means to base your prayer on God's promises. Faith must have an object: We cannot believe without something to believe in. There are people who say, "Just believe and you will receive it!" But they are greatly mistaken. In every situation you need a specific promise of God on which you can base your faith.

The most wonderful thing is that such promises are always to be found:

- For the lonely, *"...I am with you alway..."* (Matthew 28:20).

- For the weak, *"...my strength is made perfect in weakness..."* (2nd Corinthians 12:9).

- For the anxious, *"Casting all your care upon him; for he careth for you"* (1st Peter 5:7).

- For those who are troubled, *"...neither be ye sorry; for the joy of the LORD is your strength"* (Nehemiah 8:10).

- For the sick, *"...I am the LORD that healeth thee"* (Exodus 15:26).

For every *specific* situation, God has given a *specific* promise so that you can base your faith *specifically* on God's Word. Why do you not pray boldly in faith? *"...without faith it is impossible to please him..."* (Hebrews 11:6). Your inner battle comes from the fact that God's promises contradict what you feel, sense and see. But prayer is the highest expression of faith. You no longer let yourself be bound by the visible, but you let yourself be guided by the invisible. **Unbelief believes what it sees, faith sees what it believes.**

By faith, we see the almighty Lord. By faith, we see His working. By faith, we see the showers of blessings which He wishes to pour out. By faith, we see thousands upon thousands of sinners repent.

In believing prayer, we accept His promise as reality, although we do not as yet see the fulfillment. John testifies, *"And whatsoever we ask, we receive of him, because we keep his commandments, and do those things that are pleasing in his sight"* (1st John 3:22).

Faith can break through iron and can grasp God's omnipotence. Child of God, begin to lean on the promises of God in believing prayer and you will experience miracles! Naturally, this is contrary to our human logic and our understanding. God has destroyed the wisdom of men. God does not work logically. In His sight you must become as a child. You must be able to exclaim with Isaiah, *"What shall I say? he hath both spoken unto me, and himself hath done it..."* (Isaiah 38:15). What a wonderful God! God is waiting for you to claim His promises in believing prayer!

And further: "How shall we pray?"

Perseveringly!

The Bible commands in Romans 12:12, *"...continuing instant in prayer."* This is where our emotional prayers become evident—we give up so soon! God is testing your faith when He does not answer your prayers immediately. Many lose the greatest blessings because they give up and stop praying just shortly before the Lord pronounces His blessing. Why? Because we often experience the exact opposite of what we are praying for!

If, for example, you are praying for the salvation of your child, your husband or your wife, you will sometimes see the one in question turn even farther away from the Lord, for Satan rages especially against people for whom someone is praying, because he knows that sooner or later God will answer their prayers. Therefore do not be discouraged! Be persistent even if you see the opposite of that for which you are praying, for this is when you have the guarantee of being heard!

With Submission!

If in some matter you do not know the will of the Lord, pray with all your heart, persistently, but with submission. When David faced losing his child because of his sins, he prayed as never before. It says in 2nd Samuel 12:16, *"David therefore besought God for the child; and David fasted, and went in, and lay all night upon the earth."* For seven days he prayed, then the child died.

David's servants were afraid to tell him that the child was dead. But when David realized it, he arose from the earth, washed himself, anointed himself, changed his clothes and went into the House of the Lord and worshiped. David was submissive to the will of the Lord because he knew that it must work together for his good.

Child of God in temptation, if you are in difficulty, then pray, but submissively—for which do you think is more important? That God takes away your troubles or that you learn what the Lord is teaching you through them? Pray in submission, for Romans 8:28 is true for you too, *"And we know that all things work together for good to them that love God, to them who are the called according to his purpose."*

Pray According to the Will of the Lord

"Yes," some will think now, "we must say in every prayer: 'Lord, your will be done!'" But this is not true! Only when we do not know the Lord's will in a situation do we say, "Not my will, but yours be done." But if we know the will of the Lord and still say, "Lord, your will be done," this expression is unbelief in disguise. God makes His will clearly known to us:

• By means of express promises in the Bible.
• By the leading of the Holy Spirit.
• By means of definite circumstances and happenings.

We have no right to say, "Lord, your will be done," if He has revealed His will to us. There are children of God who are continually in doubt as to whether this or that is the will of the Lord. You can immediately be healed of this if you can say, "I only want the Lord's will at any cost!" Then you can't go wrong, for your path is prepared all the way to the end according to Ephesians 2:10, *"For we are his workmanship, created in Christ Jesus unto good works, which God hath before ordained that we should walk in them."*

Then, when you see two roads before you, pray like a child about it. In the one you feel restless, so do not go that way, whereas in the other you have peace and joy, so go that way in the name of Jesus.

If you only desire to do the will of the Lord, His Spirit will lead you into all truth. You cannot be led astray, and even if you were, the Lord would bring you back because your will is in submission to His will!

It is the will of God...

- That you pray in faith.
- That you are persistent in prayer.
- That you waste no more time but that you make yourself available to Him and serve Him as a prayer warrior, praying according to His will!

CHAPTER 6

Prayer in the Spirit

"Likewise the Spirit also helpeth our infirmities: for we know not what we should pray for as we ought: but the Spirit itself maketh intercession for us with groanings which cannot be uttered" (Romans 8:26).

Now let us ask further: "In what manner should we pray?"

In the Spirit

The text we have just read indicates the purpose of prayer, that is, the Holy Spirit prays through the one who prays. We can pray in three ways:

- Intellectually—repeating what others say, with beautiful flowery phrases. Such prayers, however, have little effect.

- Emotionally—according to our feelings. But this, too, is often a flash in the pan, as it were.

• In the Spirit—because Biblical and victorious prayer is the
  work of the Spirit of God.

A true prayer comes from God, goes through the person who
prays to the object of his prayer, and returns to God. God
loves mankind tenderly and fervently. The Bible says, "[He]
*will have all men to be saved, and to come unto the know-
ledge of the truth*" (1st Timothy 2:4).

Nevertheless, the more a person sins, the more he is surrounded by powers of darkness. God speaks to him through
sorrow and blessing, but he becomes less and less capable of
hearing. God wishes to save him, but the natural man, surrounded by powers of darkness, is unable to receive the
things of the Spirit. But now God is searching for someone—
for whom? Read what it says in Ezekiel 22:30, *"And I sought
for a man among them, that should make up the hedge, and
stand in the gap before me for the land, that I should not
destroy it: but I found none."* What a shocking accusation!

We see from this that the living God is in a position to
cancel the destruction awaiting sinners, if there are people
who will stand in the gap before Him to make up the hedge—
but He finds none. How is God brought into this position? As
soon as a child of God steps into the gap and "makes up the
hedge" for the sinner who is destined for judgment, God
begins to use such a prayer warrior who stands in the gap as
a tool.

The Spirit of God begins to groan through the one who is
praying. He presses streams of light through him into the
darkness in which the sinner finds himself. Through the
praying believer, He blesses those who do not want to be

blessed and the result is that the sinner is awakened and comes into the light. He begins to hear, he is convicted, and finds Jesus!

I want to tell you with great earnestness that God has been looking and waiting a very long time for you to become a person of prayer, but He has not been able to find you. You have no time. If only you realized the unlimited ways in which the living God would work through you if you would pray.

This charge is brought against you: "I sought among them...but found none." They talk religiously, they act religiously, they are very active, but they do not pray. In your immediate surroundings, souls are heading for eternal damnation, into a Christless eternity, because you are not praying.

Your children, your relatives, and others will never be able to know Jesus if you do not become a prayer warrior in the Spirit. All great revivals in the Kingdom of God had their origin in prayer in the Spirit.

James says, *"...ye have not, because ye ask not."* Do not think that the devil is opposed to your working. You may do much in the Kingdom of God and work hard, but it is empty and without power. It brings no fruit for eternity, because you are not praying.

Have you not yet noticed that the devil is preventing you from praying? *"I sought among them...but I found none."* You are the one whom God is seeking. Will you waste your life without becoming a person of prayer? Can you not see how your preaching, your testimony, your tract distribution, your singing, your faith life in general has become a powerless waste of energy because you do not pray? God is still searching for praying believers today!

How should we pray?

Earnestly!

"...*The effectual fervent prayer of a righteous man availeth much*" (James 5:16). In the first place, God does not simply hear our *words* only when we pray, although they may be perfectly orthodox, but He proves our hearts. How earnest must our prayer be, then? Our prayer must be as earnest as our request. Is it not terribly serious when people are heading for eternal damnation? Do you not believe in the reality of hell? Is God not true? Have you fallen for the false teaching of universal reconciliation? If so, you cannot become an earnest prayer warrior.

Is it not terribly serious when the name of our God is blasphemed through many who persist in sinning? Is it not serious that the Church of Jesus Christ lies there weak and dead, when Jesus is just about to return? Pray earnestly!

Whom Does Prayer Change?

However, another question now arises: Does God change His mind in a certain matter because of our prayers? No! We can never change God and His intentions. The opposite is the case. Through earnest prayer we are changed. WE come to that inner state of mind through which God can bless us and through us others—and the world.

Your Attitude

God is always the one who blesses. For example, when sinners hear the Gospel, their sins are still upon them. They are guilty, they do not yet have forgiveness of sin. Does God not want to forgive their sin? Of course He wants to. But why are they not yet forgiven? Because they have not yet attained the proper inner attitude, namely, that of repentance. As soon as they repent, the blessing of forgiveness of sin becomes theirs.

Does God not want revival? Does God not want to send a moving of the Spirit? Certainly He wants to! He has said, *"For I will pour water upon him that is thirsty, and floods upon the dry ground: I will pour my spirit upon thy seed, and my blessing upon thine offspring"* (Isaiah 44:3). Jesus said, *"I am come to send fire on the earth; and what will I, if it be already kindled?"* (Luke 12:49). Why is there no revival yet? Because we as children of God are not in the right attitude of mind. God cannot bless because we are not right. Only when we begin to pray earnestly with one accord and humble ourselves in prayer, will the Lord begin to open the windows of Heaven and then He will give us a powerful moving of the Spirit.

Your Determination Counts

Is it God's will that we take Heaven by force? Does he require this earnestness? Yes, He wants it! In that night when Jacob held onto the angel of God and called out, *"...I will not let thee go, except thou bless me,"* did God reject him? Did He say, "This is not the way, Jacob!"? No, it says, *"And he blessed him there"* (Genesis 32:29).

When the wrath of God was kindled against the children of Israel, and He wanted to destroy the people, Moses fell into the uplifted arms of God and pleaded before the Lord. He threw himself into the gap, so that God would not destroy the people. And what did the Lord do? Did He say: "Moses, that is not the way to do it!"? No, we read in Exodus 32:14, *"And the LORD repented of the evil which he thought to do unto his people."* Child of God, you are called to pray earnestly and with spiritual power!

CHAPTER 7

Victorious Prayer

"And it came to pass at the time of the offering of the evening sacrifice, that Elijah the prophet came near, and said, LORD God of Abraham, Isaac, and of Israel, let it be known this day that thou art God in Israel, and that I am thy servant, and that I have done all these things at thy word.

"Hear me, O LORD, hear me, that this people may know that thou art the LORD God, and that thou hast turned their heart back again. Then the fire of the LORD fell, and consumed the burnt sacrifice, and the wood, and the stones, and the dust, and licked up the water that was in the trench.

"And when all the people saw it, they fell on their faces: and they said, The LORD, he is the God; the LORD, he is the God. And Elijah said unto them, Take the prophets of Baal; let not one of them escape. And they took them: and Elijah brought them down to the brook Kishon, and slew them there" (1st Kings 18:36–40).

Enemies—Conquered Through Prayer

Here we have a demonstration of a victorious prayer in the life of Elijah. In short, his prayer conquered the enemy. Who was this enemy? It was Baal and his priests—the idol and his servants. They were the ones who dragged down the children of Israel into half-heartedness. The entire land was contaminated with it. This is a picture of the demons which also surround us and with which the entire world is contaminated. These are the spirits from the abyss: Spirits of indolence, spirits of unbelief and of worldly lust, spirits of idolatry, which want to drag us down into half-heartedness towards the Lord. And now look—Elijah overcame these enemies. With what? With prayer! Oh, that we might become people of prayer! All enemies in us and around us must flee before the holy majesty of God which will be revealed through our prayer. I tell you: The God of Elijah still lives today!

The Nature of Elijah's Prayer

It was a specific prayer. Herein lies a great secret. The Lord Jesus says that we should not make many words and babble like the heathen. By this He meant that we should ask clearly and specifically for that which is in our hearts. Many live in a religious fog. They use many words in speaking to the Lord and when they arise from their knees they have already forgotten for what they have prayed. Learn to pray specifically. This concrete prayer is nothing other than counting on the present living Savior who has the power to help and to intervene right now. Elijah says, "*...let it be known this day that thou art God in Israel*" (1st Kings 18:36).

Elijah's prayer had the right motive. The deepest motive of his heart was not even primarily the salvation of the people, but the honour of God. He says, *"...let it be known this day that thou art God in Israel..."* and in verse 37, *"Hear me, O LORD, hear me, that this people may know that thou art the LORD God...."* The burning passion in Elijah's life was for the honour of God. Only afterwards does he say in verse 37, *"...thou hast turned their heart back again."*

It is good to be praying for the salvation of your wife, your husband or your child, but why do you actually want them to be saved? Perhaps you will say: "So that they will not be lost!" Then I must tell you that this is a superficial motive. Even if God in His mercy eventually does hear you, His answer will be delayed and hindered by your egoistic motives. Yes, your wife, your husband, your child must not perish. However, there are women who pray for the salvation of their husbands, while the deepest motive of their hearts is really the fact that it will not be so hard for them then, and he will come along to church with her.

View Prayer From God's Perspective

How patient the Lord is! When you pray for the salvation of your loved ones, the first compelling thought should be: "Lord, Your holy name is being blasphemed by their unsaved state. Save them, so that You will be honored and receive the reward for your sufferings."

Elijah's prayer was founded on the absolute certainty of being heard! How could he know that the Lord would hear him and answer his short prayer immediately?

He could have been put to shame before the priests of Baal. Thousands were watching him breathlessly.

I believe that Elijah's certainty stemmed from his absolute obedience to the Lord. He calls out in his prayer, *"...let it be known this day that thou art God in Israel, and that I am thy servant, and that I have done all these things at thy word."* In other words: "Lord, I am not standing here on my own initiative but I have done everything which you have told me to do, and now you must do what I cannot do."

Elijah's obedience to God is evident already from his outward actions. First, he did not dare pray in this manner before he repaired the altar of the Lord which had been broken down (verse 30). He was standing on altar-ground. This is the way we can pray victoriously: If we take this first step of obedience, if we are standing on altar-ground, on ground near the cross.

If we continually submit our old life to the death of Jesus, we may say: "Lord, I have done everything according to your Word."

The Power of a Sanctified Life

Elijah only began to pray when it was time to offer the evening sacrifice (verse 36). What a wonderful picture when we consider that the evening sacrifice was the one of the five sacrifices of the Old Testament in which no blood was shed. The evening sacrifice points us to the holy life of Jesus which required no blood of atonement. The letter to the Hebrews says, *"...we are made partakers of Christ..."* (Hebrews 3:14). We should identify ourselves with the evening sacrifice, with the holy life of Jesus, for the Lord says, *"Ye shall be holy: for I the LORD your God am holy"* (Leviticus 19:2).

The Role of Obedience

Standing at the foot of the cross and consciously living a sanctified life are the expressions of practical obedience through which the Lord also answers prayers and sends fire from Heaven. Therefore, we read in 1st John 3:22, *"And whatsoever we ask, we receive of him, because we keep his commandments, and do those things that are pleasing in his sight."*

Let me remind you that Elijah, as James says, was a man like us, but Elijah was so powerful in his prayer because he did what the Lord wanted. You know, of course, about the tremendous three-fold consequence of this prayer:

First, the fire of the Lord fell and consumed everything—not only the sacrifice—but also the hard, cold, earthly things, the wood, stones, earth, and water. How wonderful, if we learn to pray like Elijah, standing at the cross, sanctified! Then the Lord accepts our offering, and all the Earthly things (wood, stones, and earth) are consumed by His fire.

Second, through the prayer of Elijah, the blinded people of Israel recognized the Lord, for they cried out, *"The LORD, he is the God; the LORD, he is the God!"* If this hardened, religious, godless world is to see the glory of the Lord again, it needs people who can pray like Elijah.

Third, another consequence of Elijah's prayer was that at the same hour the stubborn enemies who were misleading the people were conquered and destroyed.

Because the God of Elijah lives today and is the same, I would ask: "Who wants to learn to pray like Elijah?" If you are willing, bow your knees now and dedicate yourself to the Lord!

CHAPTER 8

Life-giving Prayer

"And it came to pass after these things, that the son of the woman, the mistress of the house, fell sick; and his sickness was so sore, that there was no breath left in him. And she said unto Elijah, What have I to do with thee, O thou man of God? art thou come unto me to call my sin to remembrance, and to slay my son?

"And he said unto her, Give me thy son. And he took him out of her bosom, and carried him up into a loft, where he abode, and laid him upon his own bed. And he cried unto the LORD, and said, O LORD my God, hast thou also brought evil upon the widow with whom I sojourn, by slaying her son?

"And he stretched himself upon the child three times, and cried unto the LORD, and said, O LORD my God, I pray thee, let this child's soul come into him again. And the LORD heard the voice of Elijah; and the soul of the child came into him again, and he revived.

"And Elijah took the child, and brought him down out of the chamber into the house, and delivered him unto his mother:

and Elijah said, See, thy son liveth. And the woman said to
Elijah, Now by this I know that thou art a man of God, and
that the word of the LORD in thy mouth is truth" (1st Kings
17:17–24).

Here before us, we have a life-giving prayer. Life broke
through where the death of this world was asserting its
power. Wherever spiritually powerful people pray, the power
of the Risen One breaks through and the dead come to life.
I am speaking of "spiritually dead" people.

Let us consider more closely how Elijah prayed and the
effect of his prayer.

**First, this was a solitary prayer, for Elijah went up
alone into the attic.** There is a great secret in this. When
the Lord Jesus speaks of solitary prayer, He says, *"...enter
into thy closet, and when thou hast shut thy door, pray to thy
Father which is in secret..."* (Matthew 6:6). Life-giving prayer
is prayed in solitude.

**Second, this life-giving prayer came from a man who
had taken a burden with him into his solitude: a dead
child.** *"And he took him out of her bosom, and carried him up
into a loft...."* God wants to trust you with His burdens.

In Jeremiah 23:33, the prophet speaks of the "burden of
the Lord." This word "burden" occurs again and again in the
Bible. Prophets and men of God have carried it and have
wept over it before the Lord.

My brothers and sisters in the Lord: In your surroundings
there are "burdens of the Lord" including the burden of your
dead church, the burden of spiritually dead people, the burden of a world ripe for judgment. Who will carry it in solitude

into the Holy Place? Such burden-bearers are real praying believers. The heavier your burden weighs upon you, the more glorious the victory the Lord will give you in prayer. The greatest burden-bearer of all men and of all times is Jesus Christ, *"Behold the Lamb of God, which taketh away the sin of the world"* (John 1:29).

Third, this life-giving prayer of Elijah was an abandonment of his own comfort. 1st Kings 17:19 says that he laid the dead boy on his own bed. The prophet Elijah was certainly a man of sacrifice. He had no Earthly possessions, he had given up the comfort of this world for the sake of his service. He had only this little room, and this bed was probably his only comfort, the resting place for his tired body. But he gives up this last piece of private life for the object of his prayer. He lays the dead child on his bed.

This is a tremendous truth: Whatever costs little is worth little! To what extent are you willing to do without the pleasant, comfortable things of life and to walk the way of the cross? Oh, that we would become like Jesus as is written in 2nd Corinthians 8:9, *"For ye know the grace of our Lord Jesus Christ, that, though he was rich, yet for your sakes he became poor, that ye through his poverty might be rich."*

Your Prayer is a Sacrifice

According to the measure in which we are willing to sacrifice our own lives, also in prayer, others can become partakers of the life of Jesus. The climax of Elijah's sacrifice in his prayer was when he stretched himself three times upon the child and thus cried unto the Lord, *"O LORD my God, I pray thee, let this child's soul come into him again!"* (1st Kings 17:21).

Let us picture this: The living Elijah makes himself one with the dead child. He identifies himself with him. With this action, he really says: "Your death is my death, and my life is your life." Thus he cries to the Lord and the Lord hears and answers, and the child lives!

What a wonderful picture of our heavenly Elijah, of Jesus Christ! He who is life eternal identifies Himself with eternal death, which is what we are, *"...dead in trespasses and sins"* (Ephesians 2:1). When He hung on the cross, He made Himself one with your sin and mine, and in 2nd Corinthians 5:21 we read, *"For he hath made him to be sin for us, who knew no sin...."* And thus made one with us, He prayed for you and me, *"...Father, forgive them; for they know not what they do..."* (Luke 23:34).

Identify With the One You're Praying For

Are you a follower of Jesus? You say, "Yes!" Then you can know today the secret of life-giving prayer: Make yourself one in spirit with the spiritually-dead person. Throw yourself down before God and cry to Him without ceasing. Persevere and let your willingness to die for others be wholehearted. Many give up so soon.

In Gethsemane, He could have destroyed the enemy. When the people challenged Him to come down from the cross, He could have summoned millions of angels. But His act of dying was perfect and complete. He breathed out His life for our sakes. Jesus Christ lay in the grave for three days. The sacrifice of Elijah's life was compete as he three times stretched himself upon the child. It was a prayer of complete sacrifice. I can tell you with certainty that God longs to impart the life of Jesus to others through our willingness to surrender ourselves (see 2nd Corinthians 4:10–11).

The Power of a Complete Surrender

I believe that the reason there are so many spiritual miscarriages, despite our preaching and our prayers, lies in the two little words "not completely." Not completely surrendered, not completely crucified with Christ, not willing to dedicate one's whole life. God never does half jobs, but you are doing it in your prayer life, in your witnessing and in your walk with the Lord. I would earnestly ask you to become an Elijah—one who will carry the Lord's burdens in prayer, one who will give up his own comfort for the sake of praying, one who in prayer surrenders his life to the Lord and, thereby, to the object of his prayer. If you are willing to do this, the same will happen as in the case of Elijah, *"And the LORD heard the voice of Elijah; and the soul of the child came into him again, and he revived"* (1st Kings 17:22). The Lord wants to hear you and wants to give eternal life to many through your prayer!

CHAPTER 9

Persevering Prayer

"And the men turned their faces from thence, and went toward Sodom: but Abraham stood yet before the LORD. And Abraham drew near, and said, Wilt thou also destroy the righteous with the wicked?" (Genesis 18:22–23).

What a tremendous man of prayer Abraham was! He remained before the Lord, he persevered in prayer. That he was a tremendous man of prayer can be recognized by the effects of his prayer.

The Collision Between Darkness and Light

Due to Abraham's prayer there was a clash between the powers of light and the powers of darkness in Sodom.
When in Genesis 19:4–5 the angels came to Lot and wanted to stay the night with him it says, *"But before they lay down, the men of the city, even the men of Sodom, compassed the house round, both old and young, all the people from every quarter: And they called unto Lot, and said unto him, Where are the men which came in to thee this night? bring them out*

unto us, that we may know them." Where everything goes
smoothly and quietly, in a world which is infested with
demons, there is not enough prayer. The angels of God went
to Lot's house where they met the angels of Satan. Children
of God, why do you fear an encounter with the darkness? It
is because you are not praying! Stand still before the Lord as
Abraham did: Be steadfast! Then you will surely experience a
moving of the Spirit in your church, in your family, even in
your city! Where people are praying, God sends His powers
of light into the darkness. The person who earnestly wrestles
with and cries to God on his knees initiates a battle in the
invisible world.

**Due to Abraham's prayer, the victory of the Lord, the
sovereign power of God over the power of darkness was
revealed.** In Genesis 19:11 we read, *"And they smote the
men that were at the door of the house with blindness, both
small and great: so that they wearied themselves to find the
door."* Praise the Lord that the outcome of the battle is
already decided! Jesus is victorious! But this victory can only
become effective and visible where there are "Abrahams" who
stand before the Lord.

The victory of Jesus can be revealed in your city! May God
give us grace to bring our lazy, sluggish and comfort-loving
flesh to the cross and remain standing before the Lord until
the victory of Jesus is revealed before the eyes of all.

**Due to Abraham's prayer the man, Lot, for whom he
was praying, came into great difficulty.** *"...And they
pressed sore upon the man, even Lot..."* (Genesis 19:9). You
will experience that when you bring, by name, people who
have been laid upon your heart before the Lord and remain

standing before the Lord, these people will finally come into great difficulty, into inward and outward troubles, into sin, into conflict with their surroundings. Pray, pray, pray, that people of the world in your environment may come into difficulties! Then they will be ripe for salvation!

Through the powerful prayer of Abraham, Lot was saved. In Genesis 19:29 it says, *"And it came to pass, when God destroyed the cities of the plain, that God remembered Abraham, and sent Lot out of the midst of the overthrow, when he overthrew the cities in the which Lot dwelt."* Let us fall on our knees and repent of not remaining before the Lord.

Now, do not offer theological arguments that God has ways of finding the people whom He wants to save. I can tell you with great certainty: People in your immediate vicinity are going to their eternal damnation because you are not praying! If Abraham had not prayed, Lot would have been destroyed. If Abraham had not pleaded, Lot would have been lost. But Abraham did pray. People who pray can bring about miracles!

Through Abraham's prayer, Lot was not only saved, but a division took place within his family. It suddenly became evident who was actually saved and who was not. In Genesis 19:26 it says about the flight from Sodom, *"But his wife looked back from behind him, and she became a pillar of salt."* We must be aware of the fact that perseverant prayer brings about clear divisions. The division runs through congregations, through churches, families and marriages. Jesus says, *"Think not that I am come to send peace on earth: I came not to send peace, but a sword. For I am come to set a*

*man at variance against his father, and the daughter against
her mother, and the daughter in law against her mother in
law.*

*"And a man's foes shall be they of his own household. He
that loveth father or mother more than me is not worthy of me:
and he that loveth son or daughter more than me is not worthy of me"* (Matthew 10:34–37). If there are children of God
among my readers whose bitter experience is a division ("a
sword") between them and their loved ones since their con-
version, then be of good cheer and continue to pray, for the
Lord will carry you through. Look what the prayer of
Abraham accomplished!

What is Your Standing Before God?

Lot, who had a weak character, who had been weak-willed
and undecided, became a man not only saved through the
power of God, but also separated from all the powers of
darkness. This could only happen because Abraham had
separated himself from the very nature of Sodom. He had
testified to his attitude toward the King of Sodom earlier:
*"I have lift up mine hand unto the LORD, the most high God,
the possessor of heaven and earth, That I will not take from a
thread even to a shoelatchet, and that I will not take any
thing that is thine, lest thou shouldest say, I have made
Abram rich"* (Genesis 14:22). Abraham wanted nothing from
Sodom, and did not want to make the slightest compromise
with any kind of sin, but he lifted his hands to the Lord.

Let us examine ourselves and see to what extent our
prayer, our standing before the Lord, is genuine. When you
pray, you are turning to Him. However, you will never be

able to turn to Him victoriously in the Spirit if you have not turned away from this world, and cut through every thread of compromise. Herein also lies the secret of the tremendous effect of Abraham's prayer.

Child of God, become determined! I want to ask you earnestly to look with your spiritual eyes at your daily life and in God's light you will recognize where you are still making compromises. Cut all the bonds of compromise so that you, too, may stand before the Lord. Then your prayer will have the effect which Abraham's prayer had: A tremendous chain reaction! For not only was Lot saved, but because of Lot, because of Abraham's prayer, the entire city of Zoar was spared and saved. Lot said, *"Behold now, this city is near to flee unto, and it is a little one: Oh, let me escape thither, (is it not a little one?) and my soul shall live. And he said unto him, See, I have accepted thee concerning this thing also, that I will not overthrow this city, for the which thou hast spoken"* (Genesis 19:20–21). Abraham stood before the Lord!

CHAPTER 10

Intercessory Prayer

"...God forbid that I should sin against the LORD in ceasing to pray for you: but I will teach you the good and the right way" (1st Samuel 12:23).

The Sin of Neglect

The greatest sin of omission is the neglect of persistent intercession. When Samuel laid down his office as judge, he declared solemnly before all the people, *"...God forbid that I should sin against the Lord in ceasing to pray for you...."* All true children of God fear this sin—they pray without ceasing.

In Jeremiah 15:1, God mentions Moses and Samuel as men who stand before Him.

Noah, Daniel and Job were also men of prayer, for God mentions them in Ezekiel 14:14–17.

Elijah was a man like us, but he was a man who prayed earnestly before God, and the Lord heard him (James 5:17).

Abraham prayed earnestly for Lot, and God heard him and saved Lot (Genesis 18:22).

Hannah prayed to the Lord and wept much, and He gave her a son who became a great tool in God's hand (1st Samuel 1:10).

The mighty king of Assyria, Sennacherib, surrounded Jerusalem and Judah was in great danger. But in 2nd Chronicles 32:20–21 we read, *"And for this cause Hezekiah the king, and the prophet Isaiah the son of Amoz, prayed and cried to heaven. And the LORD sent an angel, which cut off all the mighty men of valour, and the leaders and captains in the camp of the king of Assyria. So he returned with shame of face to his own land. And when he was come into the house of his god, they that came forth of his own bowels slew him there with the sword."*

How long will you, dear brothers and sisters, continue to sin by neglecting prayer? The time is short, *"...the night cometh, when no man can work"* (John 9:4). You are to work by praying. Paul was a man of prayer. But the greatest proof of the necessity for prayer is to be found in our Lord. If the Son of God withdrew so often in order to pray, and even prayed for entire nights, how much more do we need to?

What Accompanies Prayer

Apart from God's wonderful answers to prayers, it is important to see the things which accompany prayer. In Luke 3:21 it says, *"Now when all the people were baptized, it came to pass, that Jesus also being baptized, and praying, the heaven was opened."*

Dear brethren, this is the first consequence. As soon as we pray, heaven is opened. Our life then stands under an open heaven. In Luke 9:29 we read, *"And as he prayed, the fashion of his countenance was altered, and his raiment was white and glistering."* Do you know that a true praying Christian is immediately recognizable? He bears the reflection of the glory of God!

After forty days on Mount Horeb in the presence of God, Moses came down again and his face shone so brightly that the people of Israel were afraid to look at him.

When Jesus prayed, His face was changed and His clothes became white and shining. This is a picture of the growing transformation of the child of God. To the extent that you pray, all hardness will disappear from your face. Your face will be changed—you will begin to resemble Jesus!

You will experience the truth of 2nd Corinthians 3:18 personally, *"But we all, with open face beholding as in a glass the glory of the Lord, are changed into the same image from glory to glory, even as by the Spirit of the Lord."*

Are You Being Conformed to His Image?

Sometimes we can see how married couples who live in complete harmony with each other begin to look more and more like each other, the older they become.

According to Romans 8:29 it is God's purpose that, little by little, you become conformed to the image of His Son, *"For whom he did foreknow, he also did predestinate to be conformed to the image of his Son, that he might be the firstborn among many brethren."* This will happen if you look into His face often and speak much with Him. Thus, prayer is one of the best means of being conformed to the image of Jesus. Many children of God are not yet aware of the importance of this matter.

You must be conformed to the image of Jesus. One day when you arrive on the other side, the great question will be whether or not Jesus will recognize you, whether He will find His image in you.

What does He say to those who plead, *"...Lord, Lord, have we not prophesied in thy name? and in thy name have cast out devils? and in thy name done many wonderful works?"* His answer will be, *"And then will I profess unto them, I never knew you: depart from me, ye that work iniquity!"* (Matthew 7:23). Yes, He has known them, but He has not recognized them. In spite of their religious activity and piety they were never willing to have their own nature blotted out in prayer, to die with Christ. The tragic fact remains: He is a stranger to them! *"...I never knew you: depart from me, ye that work iniquity!"*

"And as he prayed, the fashion of his countenance was altered, and his raiment was white and glistering." Child of God, pray! Seek Jesus and His light. Everything else is of no help to you.

The Importance of Separation

Indeed, we can only experience these wonderful conse- quences accompanying prayer when we go the Biblical way of separating ourselves completely! Jesus says in Matthew 6:6, *"But thou, when thou prayest, enter into thy closet, and when thou hast shut thy door, pray...."* He sought solitude. *"...he went up into a mountain apart to pray..."* (Matthew 14:23).

Why must we separate ourselves, shut the door, and find solitude? Because all of hell is mobilized against those who pray. Be on the watch for it! When you have decided to come before the Lord, there is sure to be some disturbing reaction from Satan: The telephone rings, a visitor arrives, the baby begins to cry, or you suddenly remember something that must be done urgently. Jesus experienced this. In Mark 1:35–37 it says, *"And in the morning, rising up a great while before day, he went out, and departed into a solitary place, and there prayed. And Simon and they that were with him followed after him. And when they had found him, they said unto him, All men seek for thee."*

Seek a Quiet Place of Refuge

Thus, we see that Jesus, the great Man of prayer, was pursued by restless people. Today we are surrounded by rushing, nervous people. The Scripture says, *"...study to be quiet..."* (1st Thessalonians 4:11) and *"Be still, and know that I am God..."* (Psalm 46:10). The way of the Lamb is a lonely way, a way which leads into solitude.

Therefore, I urge you: Look for a place where you can seek the Lord alone, in prayer, and let nothing and no one keep you from it, for thus says the Lord, *"And ye shall seek me, and find me, when ye shall search for me with all your heart. And I will be found of you..."* (Jeremiah 29:13–14).

God is waiting to bless you. God longs to reveal Himself to many others through your prayer. Therefore flee from activity into solitude, and as surely as the Bible is God's Word and cannot lie, so surely will God meet you and mightily reveal Himself through your life of prayer!

CHAPTER 11

The Effects of Prayer

"After these things the word of the LORD came unto Abram in a vision, saying, Fear not, Abram: I am thy shield, and thy exceeding great reward. And Abram said, Lord GOD, what wilt thou give me, seeing I go childless, and the steward of my house is this Eliezer of Damascus?" (Genesis 15:1–2).

Abraham's Successful Prayer Life

When we consider the life of Abraham, we are filled with holy jealousy: His faith, his victory, his friendship with the living God are all good examples. But all these were the result of a deeper cause. The source of life for Abraham was his strong prayer life! Only according to the measure in which you pray will your life be a fruitful life, full of victory, joy and faith. Let us, therefore, take a look at Abraham's prayer:

His prayer was always inspired by God's speaking, through God's Word. Who begins the dialogue in Genesis 15? It is the Lord! *"...Fear not, Abram: I am thy shield, and thy exceeding great reward."* Abraham's spirit of prayer is

kindled by this Word from God. It is as if the Lord's speaking
brings out all his sorrow: The personal promise which God
makes to Abraham exceeds his deep personal need, *"Lord
GOD, what wilt thou give me, seeing I go childless?"* You have
not given me any seed. And as Abraham pours out his heart,
the Lord once again fills up the emptiness with His promises.

Abraham's prayer produced faith in the Lord alone. After
the Lord had spoken to him, it says in Genesis 15:6, *"And he
believed in the LORD; and he counted it to him for righteousness."* Note well how the faith which was pleasing to God
was the result of the wonderful exchange of words between
God and Abraham: God speaks to Abraham and Abraham
speaks to God in prayer. The result: Abraham believed in the
Lord! He no longer believed in his own dead body, he no
longer believed in his aged wife, but he believed in the Lord.

What is Your Desire?

Do you want your faith to become like Abraham's faith?
Then this exchange of words must take place in your heart
also. If the Lord can speak to you, then you can speak to
Him. Pray without ceasing. This exchange of words produces
the faith which is pleasing to God and which overcomes all
things. Abraham believed in the Lord and it was counted to
him for righteousness.

Furthermore, this prayer of Abraham penetrates into the
center of God's fullness, for in verse 8 he asks the Lord,
"Lord GOD, whereby shall I know that I shall inherit it?" In
verse 7, the Lord promises to give him the land, *"...to give
thee this land to inherit it."* But Abraham also wants to know
from the Lord how this can possibly be realized, saying in

effect, "Lord, whereby shall I know that I shall inherit it? How will your promise be realized in my life?" What answer does the Lord give him? See verse 9, *"And he said unto him, Take me an heifer of three years old, and a she goat of three years old, and a ram of three years old, and a turtledove, and a young pigeon. And he took unto him all these...."* What does this mean? The Lord's only answer to Abraham's question, "Whereby shall I know that I shall inherit it?" was, "Bring Me an offering!" Abraham asks in effect, "How will you give it to me?" and God answers, "Give me everything!" This is paradoxical—but it is the secret of the realization of God's promises in your life: To sacrifice yourself and be united with the sacrificial Lamb of God, Jesus Christ, on the cross. Then will all the promises be yea and amen in your life.

In Jesus we have all fullness. How strange are the words of verse 10, *"And he took unto him all these...."* All what? Everything which the Lord required! And the Lord says to him in verse 18, *"...Unto thy seed have I given this land...."* The Lord gives him the full assurance that His promise to him will be realized. In verse 13 God says, *"...Know of a surety...."* If only you could comprehend this!

With Whom Do You Identify?

According to the measure in which you are willing to become conformed to the death of Jesus, life from above will break through in you. When Abraham brought him all these, he was simultaneously being conformed to the death of Jesus. Verse 12 says, *"...a deep sleep fell upon Abram...."* *"...the sun was going down...."* *"When the sun went down it was dark..."* (verse 17). All these were facts which accompanied

the death of Jesus Christ, for the sun lost its brightness
when He died.

In dying, He gave His eternal life for you. The fullness of
God was made available to you. You must listen to what He
says: "I will give..." Not *near* the cross but *at* the cross!

Abraham's prayer not only produced faith but also pro-
moted the *growth* of his faith. When Abraham begins to pray,
he says in Genesis 15 that he expects Eliezer of Damascus
will own and inherit his house. In his growing prayer-life,
however, he begins to expect more of the Lord. In Genesis
17:18 it says, *"And Abraham said unto God, O that Ishmael
might live before thee!"* And later he believed that Isaac, the
son of the free woman, would be his heir. We often think that
what we first expect of the Lord is the greatest possible, but
it is often only the third best, as in this case.

The Lord wants to give you much more than this. But,
"...as thou hast believed, so be it done unto thee..." (Matthew
8:13). And once again, faith grows through prayer. The person who learns to pray, also learns to believe. Abraham's
faith was nourished and grew out of his mighty prayer-life.

The Conditions for Saving Intercession

His prayer was also saving intercession, as already mentioned in chapter 9. Let us illuminate this from a different
viewpoint this time. How many would like to make such
blessed, saving intercession for their loved ones and for the
world? Genesis 18 teaches us the condition for this. In the
first place, there must be genuine communion with the Lord.
We are familiar with the story of how the Lord visited
Abraham with two angels and how they ate together.

Eating with the Lord means having communion with Him. You can only make blessed intercession if you have real communion, a living relationship with the Lord.

Abraham was able to pray victoriously for Lot and his family who were still in Sodom, the city facing judgment, because he knew God's plan. In Genesis 18:17 it says, *"And the LORD said, Shall I hide from Abraham that thing which I do?"* Then He tells him of the great cry of Sodom and Gomorrah, and the grievousness of their sin. Abraham learns about the coming judgment and intercedes with his powerful prayer.

If we do not know the plan of God we cannot make concrete intercession. Do you know God's plan for the world today? Do you understand the political events? Can you see how God's actions are pressing towards the goal in world history?

Understanding the Signs of the Times

The center of God's acts is not Berlin, Washington or Moscow, but Jerusalem. With the rise of Israel today we are experiencing the decline of the nations. The nations are ripe for judgment. The Lord Jesus says in John 15:15, *"Henceforth I call you not servants; for the servant knoweth not what his lord doeth: but I have called you friends; for all things that I have heard of my Father I have made known unto you."* God wants to make His plan known to you, so that you can understand your times, and so that you become like the one whom He describes in Ezekiel 22:30, one who will stand in the gap for the people, the country, so that He will not have to destroy them.

What did Abraham do in his powerful intercession? He juxtaposed God's will to judge with His merciful will to save. Verse 23 of Genesis 18 says, *"Wilt thou also destroy the righteous with the wicked?"* Verse 24, *"and not spare the place for the fifty righteous that are therein? ...That be far from thee to do after this manner, to slay the righteous with the wicked...."* No, prayer does not eliminate judgment, but it enables grace to break through the judgment. I would call upon you to pray, all you believers, so that a wave of mercy may pass over this Earth once more and many souls saved from Sodom and Gomorrah before the judgment comes!

CHAPTER 12

Prayer in Battle

"Then came Amalek, and fought with Israel in Rephidim. And Moses said unto Joshua, Choose us out men, and go out, fight with Amalek: to morrow I will stand on the top of the hill with the rod of God in mine hand.

"So Joshua did as Moses had said to him, and fought with Amalek: and Moses, Aaron, and Hur went up to the top of the hill. And it came to pass, when Moses held up his hand, that Israel prevailed: and when he let down his hand, Amalek prevailed. But Moses hands were heavy; and they took a stone, and put it under him, and he sat thereon; and Aaron and Hur stayed up his hands, the one on the one side, and the other on the other side; and his hands were steady until the going down of the sun. And Joshua discomfited Amalek and his people with the edge of the sword.

"And the LORD said unto Moses, Write this for a memorial in a book, and rehearse it in the ears of Joshua: for I will utterly put out the remembrance of Amalek from under heaven" (Exodus 17:8–14).

**From this victorious period in Israel's history, we first
learn that as long as there is prayer, Amalek is defeated.**
Under the leadership of Joshua, Israel fought against
Amalek. Israel, here, is a picture of the Spirit while Amalek is
a picture of the flesh. This is exactly what Galatians 5:17
says, *"For the flesh lusteth against the Spirit, and the Spirit
against the flesh: and these are contrary the one to the other:
so that ye cannot do the things that ye would."* This battle in
the life of a child of God never ends.

Your Dual Personality

Every child of God has two natures, two personalities: The
awakened spirit, the seat of God's Spirit, and the sinful flesh
which refuses to do the will of God. It says in Exodus 17:16,
*"...the LORD hath sworn that the LORD will have war with
Amalek from generation to generation."* The battle goes on
and on! Every true child of God longs for the practical experience of victory over the flesh. As long as you pray, you actually have this victory. Verse 11 says, *"...when Moses held up
his hand, that Israel prevailed...."* By allowing you to become
weak in your flesh, the Lord wants to force you to pray.

The Spiritual Battle

But let us widen our view: Spiritual people battle purpose-
fully against the power of Amalek, the power of the flesh, the
power of this world, the power of Satan. They do it with the
sword of the Spirit which is the Word of God, through the
testimony of their lives. They will be victorious as long as
they are being prayed for. When Moses held up his hand,

Israel was victorious. The reason that many evangelistic campaigns end with only superficial, temporary blessings is that the hands of God's children are not lifted up. All blessing and success in the Kingdom of God flow from hands lifted up to heaven like those of Moses!

Corporate Prayer

Further, we see the necessity for a very close and definite cooperation between the one who prays and the one who fights the battle. We learn this from verse 11. Again and again, messengers ran up and down, from Moses to Joshua, from Joshua to Moses. When Moses lifted up his hand, Israel prevailed. Moses was encouraged to pray. They called to him, in effect, "Yes, keep on holding up your hands, we have the victory!" But when Moses let his hands droop, when he became tired, Amalek won. It was a close working together between Moses, who prayed, and Joshua, who fought the battle.

We of the *Midnight Call* seek this close, definite relationship and cooperation with God's people all over the world. We want to get out of the religious ruts at all costs. The victory over Amalek is certain; a breakthrough will occur in many countries, if there is definite, determined, concrete prayer help.

Fighting "Spiritual Fatigue"

Further, we learn from this passage that in communal prayer, we strengthen one another and help one another to overcome that deadly, paralyzing fatigue. Verse 12 says, *"But Moses hands were heavy; and they took a stone, and put it*

under him, and he sat thereon; and Aaron and Hur stayed up
his hands, the one on the one side, and the other on the other
side; and his hands were steady until the going down of the
sun." Moses would have had to give up if there had not been
supporting prayer help beside him. But it was there and his
hands remained lifted up to Heaven until the complete, final
victory had been won!

The Unchanging God

Furthermore, we recognize that when prayer decreases, the
revelation of the victory also decreases. It says in verse 11,
"...when he let down his hand, Amalek prevailed." Many of
God's children look back with sorrow on past times of blessing when there were still revivals, when thousands gathered
under God's Word. They acknowledge regretfully that it is no
longer so today. Why is it no longer like this today? People
say that times have changed. Even if the times have
changed, He, the eternally unchanging one, remains the
same, *"Jesus Christ the same yesterday, and to day, and for
ever"* (Hebrews 13:8).

Yes, it is true: Times change, people change, conditions
change, but He never changes. In Numbers 14:21 the Lord
says the following, *"But as truly as I live, all the earth shall
be filled with the glory of the LORD."* God's promises still
have complete validity! The victory of Jesus Christ over
Amalek, over the flesh, is still full of unlimited power. But
the diminishing of the evidence of this victory in your life, in
your family, in your church, is due only to the fact that your
prayers have diminished.

Pray Increases the Victorious Blessing

I would even go a step further. We learn from this passage that taking hold of God's promises in persevering prayer moved the Lord to make even greater promises. That means not a diminishing, but an increase in the revelation of His victory.

When Moses prayed on top of the mountain, he certainly must have claimed the promise which God had given to His people, that He *"...will destroy these nations from before thee..."* (Deuteronomy 31:3). As this promise now became living reality through Moses' prayer, God gave even greater promises, *"...I will utterly put out the remembrance of Amalek from under heaven"* (Exodus 17:14). And in verse 16, *"...the LORD...will have war with Amalek from generation to generation."* We learn from this that God longs to realize His greatest promises if we will begin to claim them in persevering prayer. God longs to let the victory of His Son become effective and visible. It is not God who has backed out, He has not relented, but you have.

Therefore, you must come out of the rut. You must learn to pray in battle and to battle in prayer. At this very moment He wants to equip you newly with the Spirit of prayer and power in prayer.

Seek other children of God who are of like mind. In Exodus 17 we see the first prayer group of three on top of the mountain, and a whole nation was victorious!

CHAPTER 13

Communal Prayer

Jesus Christ says, *"Again I say unto you, That if two of you shall agree on earth as touching any thing that they shall ask, it shall be done for them of my Father which is in heaven"* (Matthew 18:19).

The Importance of the Prayer Meeting

According to our text, the Lord has promised, in His Word, a special blessing on *communal* prayer. Where people pray with one accord, the demons have to flee! Where God's children kneel down together, the place is shaken and the angels in heaven rejoice! Thus, the prayer meeting is the heart of a church. In the fellowship which has a lively prayer-life, there is regenerating power present, life is there and people are converted!

The church is a center of spiritual life. In a church which has a weak prayer-life, everything is much more difficult, and a church which has no prayer meeting is a spiritual mortuary.

Origin of Revival

The origin of most revivals can be traced back to communal prayer. Pentecost began with a continuous prayer meeting where all were of one mind, according to Acts 1:14, *"These all continued with one accord in prayer and supplication...."* On the day of Pentecost, they were together with one accord, as it says in Acts 2:1. Then suddenly, there came a sound from heaven like the rushing of a mighty wind, and it filled the whole house where they were. They were all filled with the Holy Spirit, Peter preached his sermon, and on the same day 3,000 souls were converted!

And in Acts 2:42, we read of another prayer meeting, *"And they continued stedfastly in the apostles' doctrine and fellowship, and in breaking of bread, and in prayers."* In verse 47 we find God's immediate answer, *"...And the Lord added to the church daily such as should be saved."*

In all earnestness I would tell you we have the same God today, the same Holy Spirit and the same Savior. Where are those who want to come together to pray continuously for revival? In Acts 4:24, they were already having another prayer meeting, *"And when they heard that, they lifted up their voice to God with one accord, and said, Lord, thou art God, which hast made heaven, and earth, and the sea, and all that in them is."* And the immediate answer begins in verse 31!

A chain of blessings resulted: The place was shaken, they were filled with the Holy Spirit, spoke the Word with boldness, were of one accord, and had everything in common.

With great power, the apostles testified to the resurrection of the Lord Jesus and great grace was with them all. No one lacked anything among them. That was true revival—the fruit of a prayer meeting!

Praying Continually

In Acts 6:4 we find the resolve to pray continually, *"But we will give ourselves continually to prayer, and to the ministry of the word."* And then the immediate answer in verse 7, *"And the word of God increased; and the number of the disciples multiplied in Jerusalem greatly; and a great company of the priests were obedient to the faith."*

It is still possible, even today, for the Word of God to increase, for the number of disciples to become great, for many unconverted priests to become obedient to the faith, if we continue in united prayer. Many may say now: "I have taken part in a prayer meeting (or been a member of a prayer cell) for a long time, but nothing much has happened." I will tell you the reason: Of every prayer meeting in Acts, we read one little phrase which is often overlooked, the fact that they prayed *"...with one accord...."* They were in agreement. Jesus says, *"...if two of you shall agree..."* (Matthew 18:19).

Why Prayer Fails

Many of our prayers are futile. God cannot answer prayer if those who are praying are not of one accord. Outwardly, you may get along wonderfully with your brother or your sister and still carry around hidden criticism or a grudge against them in your heart. This destroys the power of a prayer meeting.

Oh, my brother, my sister, you are the obstacle if you are not at one with your fellow Christians. This is why Paul pleads so earnestly in Ephesians 4:3, *"...keep the unity of the Spirit in the bond of peace."* Where there is a break in unity, the devil finds entrance. Your dislike of a brother, your prejudice against a sister, your criticism of the one who is leading the prayer meeting is like a deadly poison. It paralyzes the entire meeting.

You all pray, but there is no power in the prayer, for the Lord does not hear it. It is time you spoke with the person in question. By the attitude of your heart, you are stifling the efforts of the entire group and the promises of God cannot be fulfilled. The Bible says in James 5:16, *"Confess your faults one to another, and pray one for another, that ye may be healed."*

Importance of Unity

I beg you with conviction: Make sure today that there is unity. But it could also be that you are not attending the prayer meeting of your church, or the prayer cell, because you find it too much trouble or too inconvenient. Let me tell you with all earnestness: If you as a child of God do not take part in some kind of prayer fellowship, you are a grave-digger for your church, and through your absence you are causing power from Heaven to be lost to your church, and to those for whom the church is praying.

Praying With Others

There are also believers who say they cannot pray in front of others. Some say that their mouths are sealed, but they can pray all right when alone.

If this is your case, I must tell you that either you are not born again and do not have the Spirit of prayer or else you are bound by your pride. You want to pray beautiful prayers and you say, "I cannot pray nicely." Renounce this spirit, go to the prayer meeting. Then open your mouth in the name of the Lord, stand before the Lord and not before man.

The Only Path to Clear Counsel

Time is short and the night will come when no man can work. Have you not noticed how an ever-increasing compulsion to evil is coming up from hell, that the nations do not know where to turn for counsel, that the godless are increasing? Only one thing can help, and that is a counteraction from above, a movement of the Spirit of God. This movement must be initiated through prayer!

CHAPTER 14

The Prayer of the Church

"...ye have not, because ye ask not" (James 4:2). As long as we are not willing to bring the most urgent requests before the Lord, specifically and continually, we shall not experience the answer. But as soon as we decide to become co-workers with God in prayer, wonderful things will happen. God's hand is ready to bless abundantly, but the hand of prayer must reach out toward Him to receive Him. You have not, because you ask not!

The Church as a Temple of the Holy Spirit

I would like to mention one of the most important and most urgent requests: That the Church of Jesus Christ should again become a true Temple of the Holy Spirit, filled with the glory of the Lord. According to Ephesians 2:20, the Church is *"...built upon the foundation of the apostles and prophets, Jesus Christ himself being the chief corner stone; In whom all the building fitly framed together groweth unto an holy temple in the Lord."*

In 1st Peter 2:4, God's children are told to assemble themselves as living stones into a spiritual house. But where is the glory of the Lord today in this Temple? Where is the power of God in the Church of Jesus Christ? Dear brethren, your religious activity cannot replace the glory and power of the Lord. Your preaching may be theologically perfect. Your singing may be very acceptable, musically speaking, but the power and the glory of God is missing. No wonder there are notorious sleepers among you. No wonder there is a stuffy, paralyzing atmosphere in your churches. You have not, because you ask not!

The great King Solomon built an astonishing Temple. Everything was marvelously organized. But Solomon knew that if the glory of the Lord did not pervade that Temple, it would be a temple of idols. Therefore, he prayed. And the result, *"Now when Solomon had made an end of praying, the fire came down from heaven, and consumed the burnt offering and the sacrifices; and the glory of the LORD filled the house. And the priests could not enter into the house of the LORD, because the glory of the LORD had filled the LORD'S house"* (2nd Chronicles 7:1–2). This is what we need!

Have you not noticed that your church becomes a house of evil spirits if the Lord is not there? There are spirits of sleep, spirits of sluggishness, spirits of unbelief, spirits of worldly lust, and lust of the eyes. I would plead with all children of God who are members of a local church: Come together in your house of God and call to the Lord unceasingly until the glory of the Lord again fills your congregation!

Producing Spiritual Growth

And this brings us to a second request, namely, that the
Church of Jesus Christ might again have the power to produce spiritual growth. Paul says in Galatians 4:19, *"My little
children, ...I travail in birth again until Christ be formed in
you."*

Half-Christians produce half-Christians. The problem of
our times is the number of miscarriages in the Church of
Jesus Christ—people who have been spiritually awakened,
but who have never broken through to a personal living faith
in Christ. Thus they are not able to produce new spiritual
children in their evangelistic efforts. They are converted, yes,
but only emotionally converted and therefore rarely find their
way into a fruitful ministry in the existing churches. Why?
Because there is no power present to bring forth spiritual
children.

I relate the story of a woman in the Old Testament: Her
name was Hannah. She was unable to have children, *"And
she was in bitterness of soul, and prayed unto the LORD, and
wept sore. And she vowed a vow, and said, O LORD of hosts,
if thou wilt indeed look on the affliction of thine handmaid,
and remember me, and not forget thine handmaid, but wilt
give unto thine handmaid a man child, then I will give him
unto the LORD all the days of his life, and there shall no razor
come upon his head.*

*"And it came to pass, as she continued praying before the
LORD, that Eli marked her mouth. Now Hannah, she spake in
her heart; only her lips moved, but her voice was not heard:
therefore Eli thought she had been drunken"* (1st Samuel
1:10–13). In this prayer, Hannah suffered the birth pains for

her entire nation, for through her prayers not only was Samuel born, but also a man of God was raised up who led his nation to the Lord. This prayer of Hannah was at first rejected by the religious authority in the person of Eli, the High Priest. It was discredited because he thought she was drunk! It is just that way today. Where are the Hannahs among you who pray and weep before the Lord until in your midst children like Samuel are born? I would remind you with all earnestness: Today there is little power in the Church of Jesus Christ to bring forth children. I beg you to consecrate yourself to the Lord like Hannah in this sacred work of prayer and weep before His face, even if the religious or church authorities reject it and call it nonsense.

Preparing to Meet the Groom

Then I see a third pressing request for our time: The preparation of the bride, the Church, for her meeting with the heavenly Bridegroom, Jesus Christ. This preparation only takes place through watching and praying. Jesus says in Luke 21:36, *"Watch ye therefore, and pray always, that ye may be accounted worthy to escape all these things that shall come to pass, and to stand before the Son of man."*

What do you think our Lord Jesus is doing on His Father's throne for His own? Romans 8:34 says that He is at the right hand of God and is interceding for us. Hebrews 7:25 says that He ever lives to make intercession for us. Jesus will pray for us up to the moment when He comes to meet His bride.

How wonderfully this is portrayed for us in Genesis 24:63–65, *"And Isaac went out to meditate in the field at the* eventide: and he lifted up his eyes, and saw, and, behold, the camels were coming. And Rebekah lifted up her eyes, and when she saw Isaac, she lighted off the camel.

"For she had said unto the servant, What man is this that walketh in the field to meet us? And the servant had said, It is my master: therefore she took a vail, and covered herself." Rebekah, persuaded by Eliezer, Abraham's servant (a picture of the Holy Spirit), is travelling to meet Isaac. Her thoughts are occupied with the bridegroom. And Isaac, as though attracted by her willingness, goes to meet her, praying, although he does not see her as yet. Oh, I can imagine Rebekah's feelings as she travelled toward Isaac, praying much, so that she was ready immediately when he appeared, and hurriedly she got off the camel and veiled herself.

Dear Christians, I am not asking whether you are saved or not, but rather, "Are you prepared for Jesus' coming in the clouds of the air?" You can only be made ready if you let yourself be separated from all Earthly things in fervent prayer. Colossians 3:1 says, *"If ye then be risen with Christ, seek those things which are above, where Christ sitteth on the right hand of God."*

Why should we always reach out for Him in prayer? Colossians 3:4 gives the answer, *"When Christ, who is our life, shall appear, then shall ye also appear with him in glory."* Be assured, the revelation of the Lord Jesus in the clouds of the air is nearer than you think! Jesus admonishes us to watch and pray! Rebekah was ready to meet Isaac. She did not sleep on her camel. You, too, are to be ready to meet the Lord when He comes!

CHAPTER 15

The Substitutionary Prayer of Repentance

"... his windows being open in his chamber toward Jerusalem, he kneeled upon his knees three times a day, and prayed, and gave thanks before his God, as he did aforetime" (Daniel 6:10).

What kind of prayer did Daniel pray? As we consider this man of God who experienced such great things with the Lord, we shall notice the three most outstanding characteristics of his prayer.

Characteristic#1–Confession

He acknowledged and confessed in his prayer before God the collective guilt of God's people, *"We have sinned, and have committed iniquity, and have done wickedly, and have rebelled, even by departing from thy precepts and from thy judgments: Neither have we hearkened unto thy servants the prophets, which spake in thy name to our kings, our princes,* and our fathers, and to all the people of the land" (Daniel 9:5–6).

"O Lord, to us belongeth confusion of face, to our kings, to our princes, and to our fathers, because we have sinned against thee" (verse 8). This is a decisive factor in prayer for revival. We must recognize that we live in time. We can observe the past, future and present, but God is eternal. For Him the past and the future are present. A thousand years are for the Lord as one day, and one day as a thousand years.

Unconfessed sins of the people of God in the past cast a shadow, even a curse, on this generation of God's children. They have a paralyzing effect. Let us not underestimate the righteousness of God! Only thorough repentance, even over the sins of our fathers, even over the sins of others, makes room for the Spirit of God through the cleansing power of the blood of Jesus Christ.

This is true concerning the sins of parents and forefathers. The patriarchs of the Old Testament had much light in this respect. We read, *"I the Lord thy God am a jealous God, **visiting the iniquity of the fathers** upon the children unto the third and fourth generation of them that hate me"* (Exodus 20:5, 34:7, Numbers 14:18) [emphasis ours].

Many children suffer bitterly from the sins of their parents and grandparents. I can imagine that among my readers there are children of God who, in spite of the fact that they are Christians, are constantly being plagued by other spirits, by spirits of depression, unclean spirits or even by spirits of blasphemy. In the most sacred moments terrible thoughts come to them.

If you have not committed occult sins, it could be that
your parents or grandparents have and that they have not
repented of these. May I suggest to you: Do as Daniel did
and confess before the Lord, "We and our fathers have
sinned before you."

Your flesh and blood is just the same as that of your
father and your forefathers. God's righteousness is perfect.
Repent of unacknowledged sins in your own life and in the
entire family. Claim the power of the blood of Jesus Christ.
Then by praying in the name of Jesus Christ you may boldly
renounce every spirit of depression, every unclean spirit or
spirit of blasphemy and untruthfulness. The precious blood
of Jesus is powerful enough to break the line of the curse in
your family and to transform it into a line of blessing.

Many children of God forget that their salvation experience is like that of the Hebrews when they conquered the
land of Canaan. We must conquer it step by step in faith and
say to the enemy, "Be destroyed in the name of Jesus!"

We have become lazy, comfortable Christians. We sigh
over bondages and say, "This is something I have inherited
and just have to live with." But the victory of Jesus is unlimited if only you will claim the land of salvation through definite and genuine repentance of your own sins and those of
your whole family.

Characteristic#2–A Right Heart Attitude

In Daniel 10:12, we see that Daniel's prayer was a desire to
"...*set thine heart to understand....*" Only when the Lord sees
that we are praying not only with our mouth, not only as a
work of the flesh, not only with our mind, but that we are

also praying from the bottom of our heart, then the answer is immediately on the way even if we do not yet see it. The Lord says in Daniel 10:12, *"...Fear not, Daniel: for from the first day that thou didst set thine heart to understand, and to chasten thyself before thy God, thy words were heard, and I am come for thy words."*

There is a great secret here. You may pray religiously, you may speak the language of Canaan perfectly, but the Lord longs to make the answer to your prayers a reality. Yet He can do this only if you desire the fulfillment with all your heart and at all costs like Daniel. Let me remind you once more of the Word, *"...ye shall seek me, and find me, when ye shall search for me with all your heart"* (Jeremiah 29:13). O' God, give grace that my whole heart and being may seek You!

Characteristic#3–Ignore the Circumstance

The third characteristic of Daniel's prayer was that he was steadfastly swimming against the tide, so to speak, even ignoring the danger of death.

When King Darius, because of Daniel's enemies, forbad under penalty of death that anyone should pray for thirty days, except to the King, we should study Daniel's reaction, *"Now when Daniel knew that the writing was signed, he went into his house; and his windows being open in his chamber toward Jerusalem, he kneeled upon his knees three times a day, and prayed, and gave thanks before his God, as he did aforetime"* (Daniel 6:10). Daniel did not allow himself to be kept from prayer by fear of the enemy. He risked his own life in order to be able to pray.

Daniel defied the den of lions! The result was that he was confronted with these lions for a whole night. Yes, if you risk your own life in order to persevere in prayer, if the threatening of the enemy no longer frightens you, then you will also be confronted by the lion who stalks about roaring and seeking whom he may devour. But then you will experience the same as Daniel. The wicked one will not be able to touch you!

On the contrary, risk it, let Satan roar, let hell be in a turmoil! But pray on at all costs, for the Lord is near! Pray on, He is helping you! Pray and pray on—it will come to pass—pray and you will see miracles! Instead of the enemy triumphing, the name of the Lord was glorified through Daniel in that King Darius praised the One true God (Daniel 6:26–28).

Angelic Assistance to Those in Prayer

The second result of Daniel's prayer was that he was not only confronted with the powers of darkness, but also that the messengers of light, the angels of God, assisted him, surrounded him and strengthened him and gave him deep insight into God's plan for the world.

The secret of Daniel's power, perseverance, wisdom, and courage was his prayer life. Therefore, I pray to the God of Heaven that you, too, might become such a person of prayer (Daniel 6:23).

CHAPTER 16

The Power of Prayer

"Call unto me, and I will answer thee, and shew thee great and mighty things, which thou knowest not" (Jeremiah 33:3).

What a mystery the unlimited power of prayer is! I hesitate to speak of it because I am incapable of putting into words the unlimited omnipotence of God which is revealed to those who pray. Let's approach the center of this divine mystery with a few simple questions.

Why Do We Need to Pray?

Because God the Father tells us to, *"...call upon me in the day of trouble: I will deliver thee, and thou shalt glorify me"* (Psalm 50:15). Apart from the fact that the Lord takes to heart our cries concerning our outward troubles, the one who begins to read His Word with an open and honest heart will also inevitably come into inward difficulties. And this is when the Father says to us, *"...call upon me in the day of trouble...."*

Because God the Son urges us to, *"And he spake a parable unto them to this end, that men ought always to pray, and not to faint"* (Luke 18:1). *"Ask, and it shall be given you; seek, and ye shall find; knock, and it shall be opened unto you"* (Matthew 7:7). The Son of God urges us to pray increasingly: "Ask" is a passive asking. "Seek" is already an earnest persevering. "Knock" means coming into the very presence of God until He opens the door into the inner sanctuary.

Because God the Holy Spirit wants to pray through us, *"Likewise the Spirit also helpeth our infirmities: for we know not what we should pray for as we ought: but the Spirit itself maketh intercession for us with groanings which cannot be uttered"* (Romans 8:26). Thus, when the triune God encourages us to pray, He also gives us His promise that He will bring it to pass.

The Spirit Himself intercedes for us with unutterable groanings. How can you continue any longer in your neglect of prayer, when God urges you so earnestly to pray? In addition to this urging, He promises that He will do it through you! *"Faithful is he that calleth you, who also will do it"* (1st Thessalonians 5:24). If God has told us that we should pray, three things are necessary for us: first, prayer; second, prayer; and third, prayer!

Why is Prayer a Power?

Because when you pray, three people immediately become involved: God, Satan and yourself.

The eternal God acts. He has solemnly committed Himself to answer the prayer of His children.

- He hears, *"...the LORD will hear when I call unto him"* (Psalm 4:3).
- He answers, *"...I will surely hear their cry"* (Exodus 22:23).
- He refreshes, *"They looked unto him, and were lightened: and their faces were not ashamed"* (Psalm 34:5).
- He gives great strength, *"In the day when I cried thou answeredst me, and strengthenedst me with strength in my soul"* (Psalm 138:3).
- He fulfills, *"He will fulfil the desire of them that fear him: he also will hear their cry, and will save them"* (Psalm 145:19).
- He anticipates the request, *"...Before they call, I will answer..."* (Isaiah 65:24).
- He reveals, *"...and shew thee great and mighty things, which thou knowest not"* (Jeremiah 33:3).

For this reason it is much more important to find Him in prayer than to bring many requests to Him, before you have even found Him (Ecclesiastes 5:1). When you find Him, you already have the answer to your prayer, *"...ye shall search for me with all your heart and I will be found of you..."* (Jeremiah 29:13–14).

Perhaps you have a prayer list so that you can faithfully bring your requests before the Lord without forgetting any, and this is good and right. But remember, He whose eyes are like flames of fire, proves your heart in the first place to know whether you are seeking Him with all your heart. When you know, "Heaven is now open over me," you will have such a flood of requests that your words will hardly be able to keep pace.

Satan Begins His Violent Opposition

The invisible world of darkness gets into a state of turmoil and alarm whenever a man or a woman begins to pray (Ephesians 6:12 and Revelation 12:12). The person who prays is even more likely to come under attack because of today's greatly increased satanic activity. This is by means of an invasion of spirits from below, which is all due to the Lord's imminent return.

But because the powers of destruction are active as never before, our prayer-life must increase, otherwise we shall not survive. We shall slowly but surely yield to temptation.

But the Holy Spirit initiates a counter-action to the work of Satan. You are drawn into the realm of God's power. Yes, something wonderful happens to your personality when you pray. Do you become stronger?

No, on the contrary, weaker in that you rely on the living God! But while you are praying your weakness is united with His unlimited, all-powerful strength. Joy breaks through in your heart, *"...when I am weak, then am I strong"* (2nd Corinthians 12:10). *"I can do all things through Christ which strengtheneth me"* (Philippians 4:13). *"In the day when I cried thou answeredst me, and strengthenedst me with strength in my soul"* (Psalm 138:3). Tell me, why do you allow yourself to be so deceived by Satan that you do not pray?

Who Experiences the Power of Prayer?

Those who have been separated. Let us look at the impressive examples of three personalities from the Old Testament whose names all begin with "J."

• **Jacob.** In his great need, he was deprived of his own ability. When Esau threateningly approached him with four hundred men, all Jacob's calculations did not help him. He had only the word of the Lord on which he could rely, and he claimed it twice in his prayer which became more and more victorious, climaxing in the complete victory of Peniel, *"...the LORD which saidst unto me..."* (Genesis 32:9). *"And thou saidst..."* (verse 12). He was separated from his possessions, for when he came to the river Jabbok, he left everything which he had and remained alone. He even allowed himself to be separated from his family and children (verses 22–25). Then his victorious wrestling in prayer began, *"...I will not let thee go, except thou bless me"* (verse 26). Do you see what I mean? Only the one who is really separated experiences the unlimited power of prayer.

• **Jabez.** *"And Jabez called on the God of Israel, saying, Oh that thou wouldest bless me indeed, and enlarge my coast, and that thine hand might be with me, and that thou wouldest keep me from evil, that it may not grieve me! And God granted him that which he requested"* (1st Chronicles 4:9). This man was separated from fatal self-satisfaction.

In his family's genealogy, he stands out as being different. *"...Jabez was more honourable than his brethren..."* (1st Chronicles 4:9). He senses that the unlimited power of God will be revealed for him even more if he will only pray and he cries, *"...Oh that thou wouldest bless me indeed, and enlarge my coast, and that thine hand might be with me...."*

We are all afflicted with the paralyzing thought that God's power might be limited. This is pictured in 1st Chronicles

17, where David wants to build a house for God. He wishes to limit His infinite, eternal majesty to four walls, and the Lord sends him the message, *"...Thou shalt not build me an house to dwell in"* (1st Chronicles 17:14).

Even Solomon confesses later, after he has built a Temple for the Lord, *"...behold, heaven and the heaven of heavens cannot contain thee; how much less this house which I have built!"* (2nd Chronicles 6:18).

Psalm 78:41 describes how Israel tempted God and, *"...limited the Holy One of Israel."* Do not try to build the Lord a house with your limited faith! Do not limit the Holy One of Israel! We are living in a limited house which the Lord has built for us but He will gladly widen its walls, its borders, if we will only pray. David recognized this fact in the presence of God, *"For thou, O my God, hast told thy servant that thou wilt build him an house: therefore thy servant hath found in his heart to pray before thee"* (1st Chronicles 17:25).

Let yourself be separated from your self-satisfaction, break out to the right and to the left and call to Him, "Oh, that thou wouldest bless me, and enlarge my coast, and that thine hand might be with me!" Child of God, break away, away from the limitations of your shortsighted self! The Lord wants to widen your borders (enlarge your coast) worldwide! *"...And God granted him that which he requested"* (1st Chronicles 4:10).

- **Jehoshaphat.** *"O our God, wilt thou not judge them? for we have no might against this great company that cometh against us; neither know we what to do: but our eyes are upon thee"* (2nd Chronicles 20:12). This man was separated from his own power. In view of the great army of the children of Ammon and Moab, he confesses before the Lord:

- His lack of strength: *"...we have no might...."*
- His lack of wisdom: *"...neither know we what to do...."*
- His reliance upon the Lord alone: *"...but our eyes are upon thee."*

Although weak, wretched and desperate, we may yet be princes in prayer!

Without strength? Yes, I am powerless, but because of this I am even more dependent upon His strength!

Without wisdom? That is me—but because of this I can count on His infinite wisdom so much the more.

And so we have seen that real prayer is an expression of the greatest dependence on Him alone. But only those who are completely separated and freed can become dependent.

Unlimited in scope, this bountiful Promised Land lies open to you if you will allow yourself to be separated from your own ability, your possessions, from the flesh, from self-satisfaction, from your own strength and from your presumptuous manner of knowing better. Then you have nothing left—and yet you have everything. You lose yourself but you find Him! Your own nature is broken but you have broken through to Him after being separated from the things which bind you. The more you are separated from all Earthly, temporal things, the more intimately you will be bound to Him, the Eternal One. He that hath ears to hear, let him hear!

Who Won't Experience Prayer Power?

• **Stubborn, irreconcilable people.** When Hebrews 12:14 says, *"Follow peace with all men, and holiness, without which no man shall see the Lord,"* it refers, without any doubt, to the day of Jesus' return when we shall see Him as He is.

But it is also true for us today. No one can see the Lord, see Him and experience Him in prayer, if he does not pursue peace with all men. Such a person would be unclean in his nature because he tolerates a root of bitterness in his heart. He also makes others unclean through it (Hebrews 12:15). So he is not able to pray with power. Jesus says, *"And when ye stand praying, forgive, if ye have ought against any: that your Father also which is in heaven may forgive you your trespasses"* (Mark 11:25). Will you not be reconciled today with your neighbor or your relative? Forgive him for Jesus' sake for you too have been forgiven much!

• **Those who have fallen away from the Lord.** One who has fallen away is unable to pray victoriously. *"God setteth the solitary in families: he bringeth out those which are bound with chains: but the rebellious dwell in a dry land"* (Psalm 68:6). *"For the froward* [the rebellious] *is abomination to the LORD* (Proverbs 3:32). In the German Bible, both these verses quite clearly refer to those who have fallen away, to backsliders. What is a backslider? It is a child of God who has departed from his decisive stand for the Lord, *"Remember therefore from whence thou art fallen, and repent, and do the first works; or else I will come unto thee quickly, and will remove thy candlestick out of his place, except thou repent"* (Revelation 2:5). From what works have you fallen?

- **From prayer in your "closet."** The more negligent you are of this work, the less desire you will have to pray. Has your prayer life become increasingly superficial and hurried? If so, it is because you have fallen away, you are a backslider!

- **You allow trivialities to keep you from the prayer meeting which you used to attend so faithfully.** Is this true of you? Then in God's eyes you are a backslider!

- **You have become negligent about the earnest reading of the Scriptures.** You can no longer say with Job, *"Neither have I gone back from the commandment of his lips; I have esteemed the words of his mouth more than my necessary food"* (Job 23:12). You wayward child of God, come back! For as one who has fallen away you are praying without power, like a Pharisee. Yes, you are praying, but it bypasses the Lord. With deep sorrow I often sense in a fellowship that the prayers of many believers receive no "Amen" from the Heavenly sanctuary. To them, heaven is closed.

- **The Power of Prayer.** It is available to you, and yet you do not have it. I ask: does God get tired? No, Scripture says, *"...the everlasting God, the LORD, the Creator of the ends of the earth, fainteth not, neither is weary..."* (Isaiah 40:28). And yet, those who have fallen away make Him weary— those whom He constantly bids to become women and men of prayer, but who can no longer hear His voice, because they have backslidden. He says, *"...I am weary to bear them"* (Isaiah 1:14).

Called to Pray

You are making Him weary, if you pray with a wayward heart, *"...yea, when ye make many prayers, I will not hear..."* (Isaiah 1:15). Doe God tire? Yes, because of your sins, He does tire of them, *"...thou hast made me to serve with thy sins, thou hast wearied me with thine iniquities"* (Isaiah 43:24).

Are you aware that with this attitude of heart you are despising the power of prayer which God has made available to you? How long will you remain in this state? Today, if you hear His voice, do not harden your heart! Confess to Him your condition! I can assure you that He wants to make you a powerful person of prayer. His blood will also cleanse away your sin!

CHAPTER 17

The High Priestly Prayer

"These words spake Jesus, and lifted up his eyes to heaven, and said, Father, the hour is come; glorify thy Son, that thy Son also may glorify thee" (John 17:1).

When we consider this prayer, we are standing on holy ground. Throughout John's Gospel, we see the Son of God as a prophet. He speaks to the people that which the Father commands Him to say.

But now in John 17, we see Jesus as a High Priest in the reverse position. Instead of turning from the Father to His disciples, He turns from His disciples towards the Father.

The word "priest" means "one who brings near." As we read this prayer of our Lord, we are brought very near to the presence of the Father, for this is the perfect prayer. It is all-embracing.

• **Worship.** In addressing His Father, He worships Him as He mentions His attributes. He says, for instance, in verse 11,

"*...Holy Father...,*" and in verse 25, "*...righteous Father....*" In verse 1, He simply says, "*...Father, the hour is come; glorify thy Son....*" He reveals, therewith, the love of the Father for His child, saying in effect, "Father, your Son is here!"

- **Intercession.** In this perfect prayer, we also find powerful intercession. Jesus prays for His disciples.

- **Thanksgiving.** The prayer resounds with thanksgiving to the Father in the sentence which Jesus repeats again and again, "*...those whom thou hast given me....*" It is inevitable that through this perfect prayer of the Son of God, the outworkings are also perfect, for in His brief confession before the Father there echoes the central message of the Gospel, and any who will hear it see in it the only way to eternal life, "*And this is life eternal, that they might know thee the only true God, and Jesus Christ, whom thou hast sent*" (verse 3).

John 17–The Model Prayer

Just like this prayer of the Lord Jesus, our prayer must also contain these three elements: worship, intercession and thanksgiving. Then your prayer too, if it is sanctified, will radiate life. It will convey to your surroundings the clear, central message of the Gospel, as Jesus did in His confession, "*This is life eternal, that they might know thee the only true God, and Jesus Christ, whom thou hast sent.*"

I would like to put it another way: Sanctified, perfect prayer, as Jesus' prayer was, calls out with holy passion to the ends of the Earth, "*This is life eternal, that they might know thee the only true God, and Jesus Christ, whom thou hast sent."* No one can pray in the power of the Spirit without also becoming a missionary!

The Secret of Jesus' Riches and Fullness

What else can we discover in Jesus' prayer? First of all, He discloses the secret of His riches, His fullness. Didn't the Lord Jesus become poor? Of course He did! We read in 2nd Corinthians 8:9, *"For ye know the grace of our Lord Jesus Christ, that, though he was rich, yet for your sakes he became poor, that ye through his poverty might be rich."* And yet in Him was such an indescribable fullness of God.

The three short years of His ministry were accompanied by streams of life, of power and of the glory of God. The Scriptures even say of Him in Colossians 2:9, *"For in him dwelleth all the fulness of the Godhead bodily."* What power of love! What power in preaching! What endless patience! What perfect holiness and purity radiated from His being! What wonderful words He spoke! Yet now in this prayer we make the surprising discovery: Jesus had nothing, but what His Father gave Him.

What the Father Gave Jesus

The words "given," or "gavest" occur 16 times in this prayer. What had the Father given Him? All that we have just mentioned. Jesus says in verse 2, *"As thou hast given him power...."* In Himself, He was weak. All His revelation of power was from the Father alone. In verse 4 He says, *"...I have finished the work which thou gavest me to do."* This tells us that Jesus did nothing and desired to do nothing, but the work which the Father gave Him to do. For this reason, He was not rushed or tense. He had complete inner peace. And yet His work was immeasurably fruitful because it was the work of the Father.

In verse 8 He testifies that the Words He gives to the people are, *"...the words which thou gavest me...."* How amazing! That is why Jesus did not speak much. But the words He did speak were "spirit and life" as He testified, because they were the words of the living God, *"...the words which thou gavest me...."*

Seven times in His prayer our Lord emphasizes that we, His followers, were given Him by God:

- *"...as many as thou hast given him"* (verse 2).
- In verse 6 twice, *"...which thou gavest me out of the world... ...thou gavest them me...."*
- Those *"...them which thou hast given me; for they are thine"* (verse 9).
- *"...keep through thine own name those whom thou hast given me..."* (verse 11).
- *"...I kept them in thy name: those that thou gavest me..."* (verse 12).
- *"Father, I will that they also, whom thou hast given me, be with me where I am..."* (verse 24).

My heart was deeply moved as I read this. Seven times He mentions you and me! We are God's gift to Jesus! First He gave Jesus for us, *"For God so loved the world, that he gave his only begotten Son...,"* and then He gave us to Jesus!

The fact that He mentions us seven times here shows how very seriously the Lord takes you and me. You are precious and valuable to Him. He has bought you with His own blood.

We talk much about the glory of the Lord Jesus but here too the Lord emphasizes, *"...the glory which thou gavest me I have given them..."* (verse 22), and *"...that they may behold my glory, which thou hast given me"* (verse 24). In other words, as it says in Hebrews 1:3, Jesus was *"...the brightness of his glory...."* This means that He revealed no other glory but the glory of the Father. He did not glorify Himself.

How It Applies to Us

What dims the glory of the Lord in your life? Your self-glory, self-preoccupation and your egotism. It is this same pious self-glory which quenches the glory of God in us.

It is striking that while Jesus was on Earth, only those who were stripped of their own glory recognized the glory of God in Him and broke down in tears. These were the publicans and sinners. The religious people were blind to His glory, for in their eyes He was despised.

The Lord considers it of utmost importance that we know that everything was given to Him by the Father. In verse 7 He says, *"Now they have known that all things whatsoever thou hast given me are of thee."*

When will you learn, then, that you have nothing, but He has everything, that you can do nothing, but He can do everything? Notice how often Jesus repeats in this prayer, *"...thou hast given me...."* Jesus had nothing. He was the poorest of all and yet the richest. He drew continually upon the resources of God. Paul also grasped this as he called out later, *"As unknown, and yet well known; as dying, and, behold, we live; as chastened, and not killed; As sorrowful, yet alway rejoicing; as poor, yet making many rich; as having nothing, and yet possessing all things"* (2nd Corinthians 6:9–10).

Jesus possessed all things because He possessed nothing. Jesus had nothing except that which was given Him by the Father.

Having seen in this prayer the secret of the fullness and riches of Jesus, in that He repeatedly says, *"...thou hast given me...,"* let us now consider the question, "Why could Jesus ask His Father for anything and receive it?" The Lord could never have given us the promise, *"Ask, and it shall be given you..."* (Matthew 7:7), if He had not tested and experienced it Himself. There are three reasons for this:

• **The first is negative.** Twice He says, *"...even as I am not of the world"* (verses 14 and 16). Jesus was in the world as a man made of flesh and blood. The world was round about Him but never in Him. Therefore He could ask for anything and His Father gave it to Him because He never let Himself become attached to this world. He never received anything from the world and His desire was never for Earthly things.

That is why Paul calls to us, *"For our conversation* [lifestyle] *is in heaven..."* (Philippians 3:20), and *"Set your affection on things above, not on things on the earth"* (Colossians 3:2).

Herein lies the secret of answered prayer. The more powerfully we are drawn by the things of this Earth, the more powerless our prayer life will be, so that finally the Words of the Lord in Luke 21:21 will apply to our life, *"So is he that layeth up treasure for himself, and is not rich toward God."* Especially in this time of prosperity, which is also a time of judgment, the prayer life of many children of God is being choked.

- **A second reason that Jesus could ask all things of His Father and receive them lies in the fact that the Lord Jesus was already rich in God before He prayed.** God's resources were constantly available to Him. He expressed it in these words, *"And all mine are thine, and thine are mine..."* (verse 10). Jesus was fully aware of His riches in God or He would not have been able to say that. And He acted accordingly in prayer. He was the receiver, the Father the giver.

This is the tragedy of so many dissatisfied children of God. They have turned from the world and are trying to live a life which is pleasing to God, but they do not appropriate their immeasurable riches in the Lord.

Listen to Paul, a man who had made a radical break with the world, as he joyfully says, *"Blessed be the God and Father of our Lord Jesus Christ, who hath blessed us with all spiritual blessings in heavenly places in Christ"* (Ephesians 1:3).

My heart rejoices too: I am rich, very rich, in my God! Take a look in Luke 15 at the second son of the father. The prodigal son comes home and the father forgives him. He kills the fatted calf and has a fine robe put on him and puts

a ring on his finger and shoes on his feet. Then the other
son, the brother, comes home. He does not want to go into
the house where the celebration is being held, *"...therefore
came his father out, and entreated him,"* it says in verse 28.
*"And he answering said to his father, Lo, these many years
do I serve thee, neither transgressed I at any time thy commandment: and yet thou never gavest me a kid, that I might
make merry with my friends:*

*"But as soon as this thy son was come, which hath
devoured thy living with harlots, thou hast killed for him the
fatted calf"* (verses 29–30). What does the father say to him
now? Exactly what Jesus said of Himself in John 17:10,
"Son, thou art ever with me, and all that I have is thine"
(Luke 15:31). In other words, "How can you complain?"

You do not ask. That is why you are so poor. John says,
*"And whatsoever we ask, we receive of him, because we keep
his commandments..."* (1st John 3:22). Are you lacking in
strength, lacking in fruit, lacking in joy? Here is the answer:
You are not aware of your constant, infinite riches in the
Lord. *"For every one that asketh receiveth; and he that
seeketh findeth; and to him that knocketh it shall be opened"*
(Matthew 7:8).

But, *"But let him ask in faith, nothing wavering. For he
that wavereth is like a wave of the sea driven with the wind
and tossed. For let not that man think that he shall receive
any thing of the Lord"* (James 1:6–7). Are you a child of God?
You say, "Yes, by the grace of God." Then you do not need to
become rich, because you are rich in Him. The one follows
the other. If you have turned away from this world, you are
then able to turn to God and you have access to His riches.

My heart rejoices, *"...whatsoever we ask, we receive of him, because we keep his commandments..."* (1st John 3:22).

Believe that God can give you what His Word promises. Look at all the goodness He has shown you during your life!

• **There is a third reason, however, that Jesus asked and received everything of the Father. It is because Jesus passed on everything He received from the Father, for His heavenly Father's glory.** This is the secret of being able to take more and more and greater and greater fullness of His abundance. Take, so that you can pass it on to others!

Did Jesus pass on what He was given? He tells us in John 17:8, *"For I have given unto them the words which thou gavest me; and they have received them, and have known surely that I came out from thee, and they have believed that thou didst send me."* This is a chain reaction: Jesus receives the words from His Father. He passes them on to His disciples. They in turn recognize that Jesus has come from the Father, and find in God their ultimate goal, which is to glorify Him, as the Lord says, *"...and they have believed that thou didst send me."*

God will gladly shower you with His fullness, and you only have to receive it. *"And of his fulness have all we received, and grace for grace"* (John 1:16), in order that you pass it on to others and His name is glorified and praised.

The Lord does exactly the same with the glory which He received from the Father. *"And the glory which thou gavest me I have given them..."* (verse 22). In other words, there are two things which Jesus passed on after He received them from His Father: The *Word* and the *glory*. These two belong together inseparably. Many believers attempt to pass on the Word of God, but it is not accompanied by the glory of the Lord. The glory is hidden in their lives. Many others do the reverse and make an effort to tell other people something about the glory of the Lord, but it is a product of their own emotions because the Word is absent.

We Must Be United With Him

Read carefully now: The Lord Jesus proclaimed the Word of God and the glory of God in such an abundant measure because He, the Receiver, was completely united with the Giver. This is the secret. We can only pass on the Word of God accompanied by His glory to the extent that we have become one with Him, one with the Word and one, thereby, with the glory of God. Jesus sums it up in the one sentence, *"...the glory which thou gavest me I have given them; that they may be one, even as we are one"* (verse 22).

Why is there so much unfruitfulness and lack of power in your life? Because, although you pass on the Word of God, it is not accompanied by the glory of God since you do not obey this Word yourself. You try to convey something of the joy and glory of God to your unsaved children and relatives, but your attempts rebound because the Word has not become alive in you. Jesus was one with His Father through His complete obedience to the faith.

Let us now, with the help of the Holy Spirit, penetrate even deeper into the wonderful mystery of this prayer.

What Does This Prayer of Jesus Reveal?

• **First, a longing for home.** This longing wells up in Jesus
as He turns to His Father. Already in verse 1 He says,
*"...Father, the hour is come; glorify thy Son, that thy Son
also may glorify thee."* He was not speaking about the cross
here. He was about to face this terrible suffering, but He
saw beyond the cross—the glory He had with the Father
before the foundation of the world. He expresses this in
verse 5, *"... O' Father, glorify thou me with thine own self
with the glory which I had with thee before the world was."*

We must not forget that Jesus, who was surrounded by
thousands of enthusiastic listeners, was the loneliest person
who ever lived on Earth, and was understood by no one.He
was a stranger on Earth and that is why He longed to return
to His Father from this sinful world. He longed for home!

Perhaps you have experienced disappointments in your
relationships with fellow Christians. Even Jesus' most
trusted disciples disappointed Him.

When Philip, who walked with the Lord for three years,
asked Him that incomprehensible question, Jesus answered
in deep disappointment and with a sad heart, *"...Have I been
so long time with you, and yet hast thou not known me,
Philip?..."* (John 14:9).

Jesus' longing for home was not selfish, but divine and
active. He wanted to go home, but not alone. He clearly
expresses His will to His Father here. In John 17:24, He
says, *"Father, I will..."*! Nowhere else in the Gospels do we
find Jesus saying so expressly to His Father, *"Father, I will
that they also, whom thou hast given me, be with me where*

I am; that they may behold my glory, which thou hast given me..." (John 17:24).

He does not stand before His Father, however, with a contrary will which insists on having its own way. No, He is willing to pay the price for what He wants. When He says, *"Father, I will that they also, whom thou hast given me, be with me where I am..."* this is backed up by His cross and His shed blood. "I will purchase them with my own life," He is saying. That is why He received and receives a rich reward for His suffering.

In the surrender of your own life you will receive a rich reward from God. Even Isaiah saw this mystery, *"Therefore will I divide him a portion with the great, and he shall divide the spoil with the strong; because he hath poured out his soul unto death..."* (Isaiah 53:12). Look at the authority with which Jesus is praying here! *"Father, I will that they also, whom thou hast given me, be with me where I am; that they may behold my glory, which thou hast given me..."* (John 17:24).

Do you want to win souls for Him? Do you want to lead lost ones to Him? Your prayer for lost souls will be answered when it is backed up by the surrender of your own life and when your longing for glory above is not so selfish. When you deny yourself for the sake of others, your prayer will be heard and you will bring forth much fruit.

- **Second, Jesus' prayer reveals the fellowship He had with His Father.** When we hear the Son of God pray in John 17 we sense a sublime serenity. There is no conflict, no unrest, no striving in Jesus' prayer.

No, He is speaking in the presence of His Father. When I hear Him say, "Father" in verse 1, it is a childlike, "Abba, Father." This expresses all the fervent sonly love and devotion, the dependence on and surrender of a child to his father. Paul says in Galatians 4:6-7, *"And because ye are sons, God hath sent forth the Spirit of his Son into your hearts, crying, Abba, Father. Wherefore thou art no more a servant, but a son; and if a son, then an heir of God through Christ."*

Look to Jesus, who speaks with His Father as a child! I experienced this with our eighth child. It was heavenly music to me! Until then this little child could only smile at me, make gestures with his hands, and cry, but suddenly I heard the word "Daddy" come from his lips. Daddy — Father! This makes my heart rejoice, for I see in it the awakening of the child's love, the desire for Dad's attention.

O' child of God, can you pray as calmly and yet as powerfully and victoriously as Jesus prayed? The one condition Jesus states in verse 2: *"As thou hast given him power over all flesh...."* In Jesus Christ you also have power over your flesh—the sinful, unbelieving, stubborn, rebellious and disobedient flesh which continually wants to alienate you from your Father and lure you from His presence.

Thanks be to God, however, who giveth us the victory, in Jesus Christ, over the flesh! The more you put into practice the victory of Jesus, the more boldly you meet the enemy in the name of Jesus, the more childlike, dependent and devoted you will be towards your Father in prayer.

- **The third thing I find in Jesus' prayer is love.** Not that
  He loves the Father, but the Father loves Him. In John
  17:23 He says, *"...that thou hast sent me, and hast loved
  them, as thou hast loved me."* In verse 26 also, *"...that the
  love wherewith thou hast loved me may be in them, and I in
  them."* Jesus takes refuge in the Father's love.

He knows that He is safe in this love even though He is only
a few hours away from the terrible ordeal where He will not
see or feel His Father's love anymore, when He will be hung
on a cross, when He will plunge to unfathomable depths and
cry out, *"...My God, my God, why hast thou forsaken me?"*
(Matthew 27:46).

Because He knows all this and sees it approaching, He
takes refuge in the unchangeable love of His Father. Jesus
says, in effect, "You love me, Father! Whatever happens, You
love me!"

I do not know through what trial the Lord has led you, or
will lead you, or perhaps you are now in such a situation.
You no longer understand His ways. You no longer understand what He is doing with you, but I can tell you that He
loves you with an everlasting love.

Afterwards you will understand, but in prayer, in such a
prayer as Jesus prayed, you can grasp it and take refuge in
this love. Jesus needed assurance of this love of the Father
in a cold, merciless, religious world, and He hid Himself in it.
The words of the classic hymn express it so well, "Rock of
ages, cleft for me, let me hide myself in thee!"

Let these three hidden things which were contained in
Jesus' prayer also be in your prayer. Be longing for Him—not

a selfish longing—but a longing to be with Him together with many others whom you have won for Him. Strive for intimate fellowship with the Father. Rest in His bosom as a son rests in the arms of his father or mother. The assurance is that He loves us!

Three Great Requests

Now we come to the three great requests of the Lord in His prayer. These requests are not concerning the world nor even His suffering, although the Lord would have had every reason to pray for these. He could have asked His Father to reduce His suffering on the cross, but He did not. Here we see into the depths of His High Priestly heart. His requests were concerning us, His followers.

- **His first request is that the Father keep them from the evil in the world (John 17:15).** Jesus sees prophetically the fatal danger for children of God in assimilating with the spirit and ways of the world and He emphasizes before the Father, *"While I was with them in the world, I kept them in thy name: those that thou gavest me I have kept..."* (verse 12) and, *"I pray not that thou shouldest take them out of the world, but that thou shouldest keep them from the evil. They are not of the world, even as I am not of the world"* (verses 15–16).

Have you allowed Him to keep you unspotted by the spirit of this world? In your family, in your business, in your school, in the rearing of your children, in your spare time, in your clothing, are you being kept from the evil? Jesus says,

"...*strait is the gate, and narrow is the way, which leadeth unto life, and few there be that find it*" (Matthew 7:14). Only a very few find and walk the narrow way, following the Lamb, this way of self-circumspection.

Moses was a man who resisted assimilation with Egypt. He chose rather to take upon himself the reproach of Christ than to enjoy the sinful pleasures in Egypt (Hebrews 11:25).

Daniel was such a man of God who swam against the tide, who resisted the spirit of the Babylonian world while all the young Israelite men allowed the spirit of Babylon to absorb them. We read, "*But Daniel purposed in his heart that he would not defile himself with the portion of the king's meat, nor with the wine which he drank...*" (Daniel 1:8). He said "No!" to the spirit of the world and his three friends followed him. God was able to bless them!

Samuel said "No!" to coexistence with Agag, the King of the Amalekites, and dismembered him before the Lord.

Paul said "No!" to the spirit of the world and exclaimed, "*But God forbid that I should glory, save in the cross of our Lord Jesus Christ, by whom the world is crucified unto me, and I unto the world*" (Galatians 6:14).

If you say "Yes!" with all your heart to the narrow way, Jesus' prayer for you has been answered, "*I pray not that thou shouldest take them out of the world, but that thou shouldest keep them from the evil.*"

- **The second great request of the Lord is, "*Sanctify them through thy truth: thy word is truth*" (John 17:17).** We could also put it this way; When Jesus says in one sentence, "*...keep them from the evil... Sanctify them through*

thy truth...," He is saying in effect, "Let them not be
absorbed by the spirit of this world, but let them become
one in us, with You, the Lord! Let them become more and
more separated, more yielded, more purified and trans-
formed through Your Word!"

Here we have the way of sanctification clearly before us,
"Sanctify them through thy truth; thy word is truth." Let the
Word of God reveal to you more of the truth about yourself
and you will come more and more into His hands. You will
disappear more in His death and Jesus will become visible in
you. This is sanctification.

*"Follow peace with all men, and holiness, without which no
man shall see the Lord"* (Hebrews 12:14). It seems to me that
many children of God are living between these two requests.
They fall prey to the spirit of this world for a time and then
they strive after holiness again in tears. These are the believers who walk in the twilight, who do not decisively step out
into the light. To these I would like to say, in the name of the
Lord, *"...How long halt ye between two opinions?..."* (1st
Kings 18:21). Do you want to follow the spirit of the Antichrist, the spirit of this world, or the Spirit of the Lord
Jesus? Do you want to be sanctified or defiled? There is a
choice to be made in your faith life. I am strongly aware that
many people are standing at the crossroads today.

The Spirit of the Lord Jesus is working mightily in prepar-
ing the Church for the Rapture, but the spirit of the Antichrist, clothed in religion, is also increasing his activity. That
is why these two requests of the Lord Jesus are of such
importance, *"I pray not that thou shouldest take them out of*

the world, but that thou shouldest keep them from the
evil...Sanctify them through thy truth: thy word is truth."

- **The third great request of the Lord is for unity.** In view
  of the misleading political, but also religious attempts at
  unity, which we see today in the ecumenical movement, it
  is important to consider the quality of unity for which
  Jesus prayed.

Two things describe the unity for which He prayed, *"That*
they all may be one; as thou, Father, art in me, and I in
thee..." (John 17:21). This is the first. How was the Lord one
with His Father? On the basis of His complete obedience of
faith. For this reason He could say, *"I and my Father are*
one" (John 10:30), and *"...the Father hath not left me alone;*
for I do always those things that please him..." (John 8:29).
This is the unity the Lord wants.

What was the nature of Jesus' obedience? *"...he humbled*
himself, and became obedient unto death, even the death of
the cross" (Philippians 2:8). It is the unity in the cross of
Calvary! Then the Lord says in John 17:21, *"...That they all*
may be one; as thou, Father, art in me, and I in thee, that
they also may be one in us: that the world may believe that
thou hast sent me." This means being one in God and Jesus,
the crucified, risen and returning Lord.

It is organic unity and not an organized unity. It is unity
in the blood of the Lamb. It is not ecumenical unity which is
an amalgamation of believers and unbelievers, which compromises with those who deny the redeeming blood of the
Lord, and who do not believe in His resurrection, thus unit-

ing Christians and antichristians. No, it is the unity which Jesus had with the Father. Jesus went even further, *"...that they also may be one in us...."* There is no unity in God, the Father, the Son and the Holy Spirit which denies the blood of the Lord Jesus. All Christian unity outside of this unity is an antichristian, ungodly unity.

Disunity among children of God is only the outward sign of their inward separation from the Lord, for whoever is one with the Lord is also one with his brother who is one with the Lord. I want to repeat that whoever is one with the Lord is also one with his brother who is one with the Lord. What a small flock it is today which finds this way of unity in the Lord Jesus, which grasps this mystery of the Church of Jesus Christ! This unity cannot be organized through "talks" and discussion. This unity exists where there are Christ-centered believers who are one in the Lamb of God.

The closer we are to Jesus, the more clearly we recognize the misleading satanic antichristian efforts to bring about unity—politically, economically, and religiously. All these will culminate in the kingdom of the Antichrist. He that hath ears to hear, let him hear!

The Consequences

What is the inevitable consequence of Jesus' three requests? He says it in John 17:18, *"As thou hast sent me into the world, even so have I also sent them into the* world." Those who believe are Jesus' messengers. Watch and pray so that you remain on the narrow way, following the Lamb! *"For yet a little while, and he that shall come will come, and will not tarry"* (Hebrews 10:37).

Finally, why did the Lord Jesus want us to hear this prayer? He tells us in John 17:13, *"And now come I to thee; and these things I speak in the world, that they might have my joy fulfilled in themselves."* Will you say "Yes!" to this message from the Word of God? Will you say "Yes!" to the way of the Lamb, the way of self-denial? Then rejoice, for Jesus prayed for you! He is even praying for you now. He will gloriously bring to completion the work He has begun in you. You are *called to pray!* ∎